# TAO TE CHING

## ALSO AVAILABLE FROM SHAMBHALA PUBLICATIONS

**Graphic Novels by Sean Michael Wilson**

The 47 Ronin

The Book of Five Rings

Bushido

Cold Mountain

The Demon's Sermon on the Martial Arts

Lafcadio Hearn's "The Faceless Ghost" and
Other Macabre Tales from Japan

Musashi

# TAO TE CHING

# LAO TZU

from the translation by **William Scott Wilson**

adapted by **Sean Michael Wilson**   illustrated by **Cary Kwok**

lettering by **Benjamin Dickson**

SHAMBHALA
BOULDER
2018

Shambhala Publications, Inc.
4720 Walnut Street
Boulder, Colorado 80301
www.shambhala.com

9 8 7 6 5 4 3 2 1

First Edition
Printed in the United States of America

∞ This edition is printed on acid-free paper that meets the
American National Standards Institute Z39.48 Standard.

♻ Shambhala Publications makes every effort to print on recycled
paper. For more information please visit www.shambhala.com.

Shambhala Publications is distributed worldwide by
Penguin Random House, Inc., and its subsidiaries.

Designed by Howie Severson

**Library of Congress Cataloging-in-Publication Data**
Names: Wilson, Seán Michael, author. | Kwok, Cary, illustrator. | Dickson, Benjamin, Letterer. |
Adaptation of (expression) Laozi. Dao de jing.
English (Wilson)
Title: Tao te ching: a graphic novel / Lao Tzu; adapted by Sean Michael Wilson from the
translation by William Scott Wilson; illustrated by Cary Kwok; lettering by Benjamin Dickson.
Other titles: Dao de jing. English (Seán Michael Wilson)
Description: Boulder: Shambhala, 2018.
Identifiers: LCCN 2018016715 | ISBN 9781611803280 (pbk.: alk. paper)
Subjects: LCSH: Laozi. Dao de jing—Comic books, strips, etc. | Graphic novels.
Classification: LCC BL1900.L26 E5 2018b | DDC 299.5/1482—dc23
LC record available at https://lccn.loc.gov/2018016715

# INTRODUCTION

The *Tao Te Ching* is one of the most influential books in human history. Yet it's not even really a book. It's a collection of eighty-one passages, written by the sage Laozi or Lao Tzu–in Chinese his name is 老子 (Old Master)–perhaps during the sixth century BCE. Or did he write the text at all? Or did he even exist? Some historians doubt it. Perhaps it was written by some other mysterious figure, or several others!

We have come to know the passages collectively as the *Tao Te Ching* or *Dao De Ching*. The meaning of the Chinese characters can be thought of as:

道
Tao/Dao–the way

德
Te/De–virtue, inner strength, or morals

經
Ching/Jing–great book or classic

So, the full title of 道德經 (*Tao Te Ching*) can be understood as "The Classic of the Way and the Power" or "The Canon of the Path and the Virtue." Or it can be understood very simply: "The Book of the Way."

The book presents a challenge, even to an experienced translator. The passages were written on bamboo strips in classical Chinese during a time when understanding the subtle meaning and nuance of characters required a considerable understanding of Chinese literature and culture. In any case, many lines are deliberately vague. Their poetical quality inspires us, but the ambiguity can leave us scratching our heads.

To further complicate things, scholars identify various versions of the texts. Lao Tzu himself almost certainly never used the title *Tao Te Ching*. It was the historian Suu-ma Ch'ien (alternatively spelled Sima Qian; 145- or 135-86 BCE) who noted that the passages are concerned with both Tao and Te, and so the book gradually came to be known by some as the *Tao Te Ching*.

The text was arranged into the present form around that time by Ho-shang Kung, who also wrote a commentary on the text and divided up the verses that focused on Tao from the others on the Te. There is also the commentary by Wang Pi (226-249 CE), which encouraged an interpretation of the texts in a way that was compatible with Confucianism.

There have also been some recent discoveries of manuscripts written on ancient bamboo, silk, and paper. In the 1920s and 1930s, more than fifty *Tao Te Ching* manuscripts were found among thousands of scrolls in the Mogao Caves near Dunhuang in Western China. In 1973, the "Mawangdui Silk Texts," from before 168 BCE, were found in a tomb in the Hunan province of Southern China, including two copies of the *Tao Te Ching* ("Text A" and "Text B") that put the *Te* section before the *Tao*. The oldest version was found quite recently, in 1993, on bamboo tablets, in a tomb in the Hubei province of Eastern China. These "Guodian Chu Slips" from around 300 BCE comprise 804 bamboo slips by various Confucian disciples; fourteen of the slips had text not found in any other version of the *Tao Te Ching*.

What exactly *is* Tao? Well, if we could give a definitive answer to that here it may be for the first time! It has been thought of as the creative principle of the universe that connects everything, from the movements of the planets to the intimate connections between people. Yet it's not a thing that can be touched or directly seen. There is no THE Tao. Just "Tao." And it's not god. It's not worshiped like a deity. As passage four tells us, Tao is an empty vessel:

. . . as empty as an empty bowl.

Yet when used, it never fills.

What is Taoism/Daoism? Perhaps at a prosaic level, it is an ancient Chinese tradition and system of philosophy and ethics that is especially important in East and Southeast Asia, but it has influence throughout the world. It is seen as a system of guidance on how to live in tune with cycles of change, to have awareness of our place within the web of Life, and to act according to the principles of *wu-wei* (*nondoing*) and *wu* (*emptiness*) with naturalness, ease, and spontaneity.

Its influence is still evident today in art, literature, and philosophy. Some think that in the dynamic between Taoist and Confucian ideas we can see the classic conflict between two opposing views: one saying that we should interfere in the order of things, the other that we should leave things to develop by themselves. This conflict is seen today in modern politics.

Indeed, Taoism is sometimes seen as having something in common with anarchism. Not the silly stereotype of violence and lawlessness, but the real approach of people organizing in a society of equals with no overbearing authority, just developing by themselves. And the Tao seems to be connected to modern ecological concerns. The focus on harmony with nature seems connected to those fighting against the exploitation of the natural world by global corporations out for short-term profit regardless of the damage to the environment. To follow the Tao we might use wind- and wave-powered energy rather than oil and coal. Instead of the burning, breaking, and boiling that leads to spilling, polluting, and global warming, we could get energy from the natural flow of water, from the milling of the free wind, or from solar panels laid out like open hands of prayer, collecting the splendid sizzling of the sun.

So, legend has it—and it may only be a legend, but then where would we be without the poetic power of legends?—that around 516 BCE, Lao Tzu decided that he had finally had enough of the corrupt politics of the Chou (Zhou) dynasty (c. 1046-256 BCE). He was eighty-eight years old and had worked for years as the Keeper of the Archives in the capital of Lo-yang. Putting that aside, he set off for the west. As Lao Tzu came, riding on a water buffalo, to the western gate of the city (or was it at the Han-ku Pass in Henan province?), the guard at the crossing, Yinxi, recognized him and said, "Great Lao Tzu—before I can let you pass I ask, I insist that you write down an account of what you have learned in your long years as a keeper of the archives. You must have a lot to pass on." To which Lao Tzu replied, "Oh, perhaps not so much. But if you insist, then I will."

So, great Lao Tzu sat down and started to write.

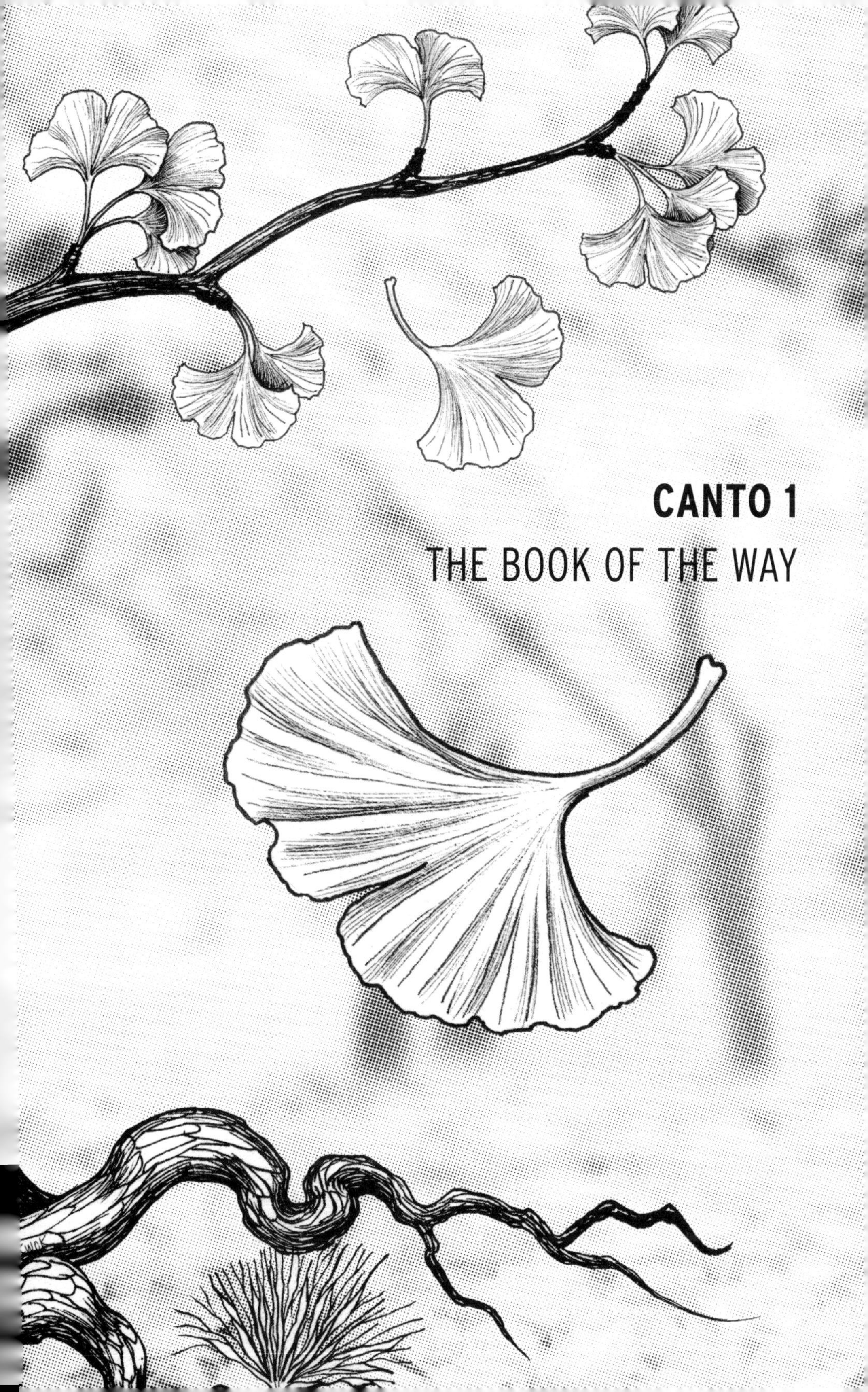

# CANTO 1

## THE BOOK OF THE WAY

# 1

The Way that can be articulately described is not the Unchanging Way.

The name that can be said out loud is not the Unchanging Name.

With your mouth unopened, and things left undefined, you stand at the beginning of the universe.

Make definitions, and you are the measure of all creation.

Thus, being forever without desire, you look deeply into the transcendent.

By constantly harboring desire, your vision is beset by all the things around you.

These two enter the world alike, but their names are different.

Alike, they are called profound and remote.

Profound and remote and again more so:

This is the gate to all mysteries.

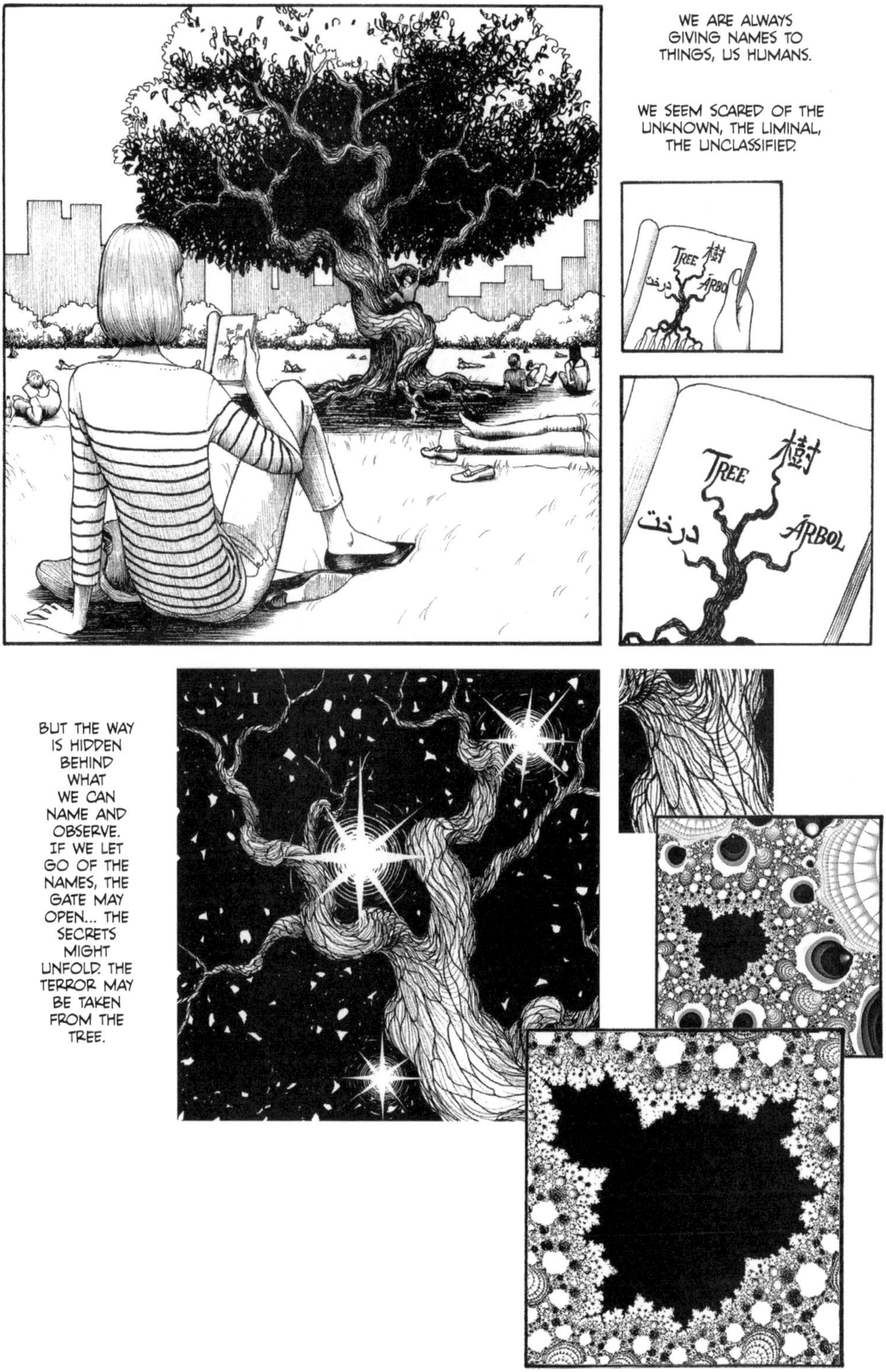
WE ARE ALWAYS GIVING NAMES TO THINGS, US HUMANS.
WE SEEM SCARED OF THE UNKNOWN, THE LIMINAL, THE UNCLASSIFIED.
TREE
樹
درخت
ÁRBOL
TREE
樹
درخت
ÁRBOL
BUT THE WAY IS HIDDEN BEHIND WHAT WE CAN NAME AND OBSERVE. IF WE LET GO OF THE NAMES, THE GATE MAY OPEN... THE SECRETS MIGHT UNFOLD. THE TERROR MAY BE TAKEN FROM THE TREE.

# 2

Everybody understands the beautiful to be "beautiful,"

But this only creates the concept of "ugly";

Everybody understands the good to be "good,"

But this only creates the concept of "bad."

There can be no existence without nonexistence;

No difficult without easy;

No long without short;

No high without low;

And without the sounds of musical instruments
and human voices, where would their harmony—
and cacophony—be?

Before and after only depend on which one follows
first.

Therefore the sage resides in nonfabrication, and
conducts himself according to wordless teachings.

All objects in the world come into existence, but he
does not judge them;

They are born, but he does not possess them.

The sage acts, but relies on nothing;

He accomplishes and moves on.

By moving on, he never has to leave.

THE UNITY OF OPPOSITES IN THIS WORLD.

GOOD/BAD... BEAUTIFUL/UGLY... HIGH/LOW.

IT MAKES LITTLE SENSE TO SEPARATE THEM
WHEN THEY ARE SO CONNECTED. THE UGLY
IS THE MIRROR OF THE BEAUTIFUL. THE
BEAUTIFUL IS THE MIRROR OF THE UGLY.

WISE PEOPLE DO NOT JUDGE
SO CASUALLY. THEY TRY TO
UNDERSTAND THE MOVE AND FLOW.

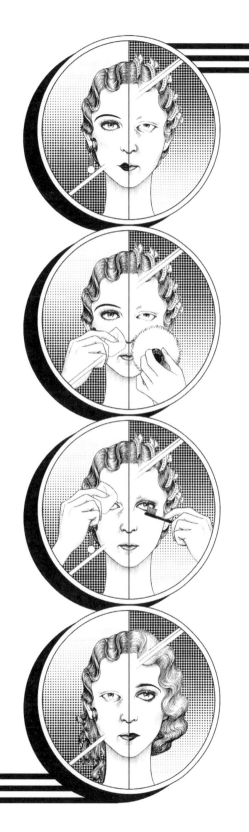

# 3

---

Do not respect the clever, and the people will not be induced to conflict.

Do not be impressed by hard-to-get material things, and the people will not be induced to covet what they lack and grab what is not theirs.

Do not stare at the desirable, and the people will not be induced to entangling thoughts.

Therefore the sage manages the flow of their activities like this:

> He empties their minds, but fills their stomachs;
>
> He weakens their willfulness,
>
> but strengthens their bones.
>
> He constantly leads the people
>
> toward less "knowledge" and less desire.

Thus, "masters" and "wise men" will not dare to act.

Act without fabrication, and there will be nothing you cannot manage.

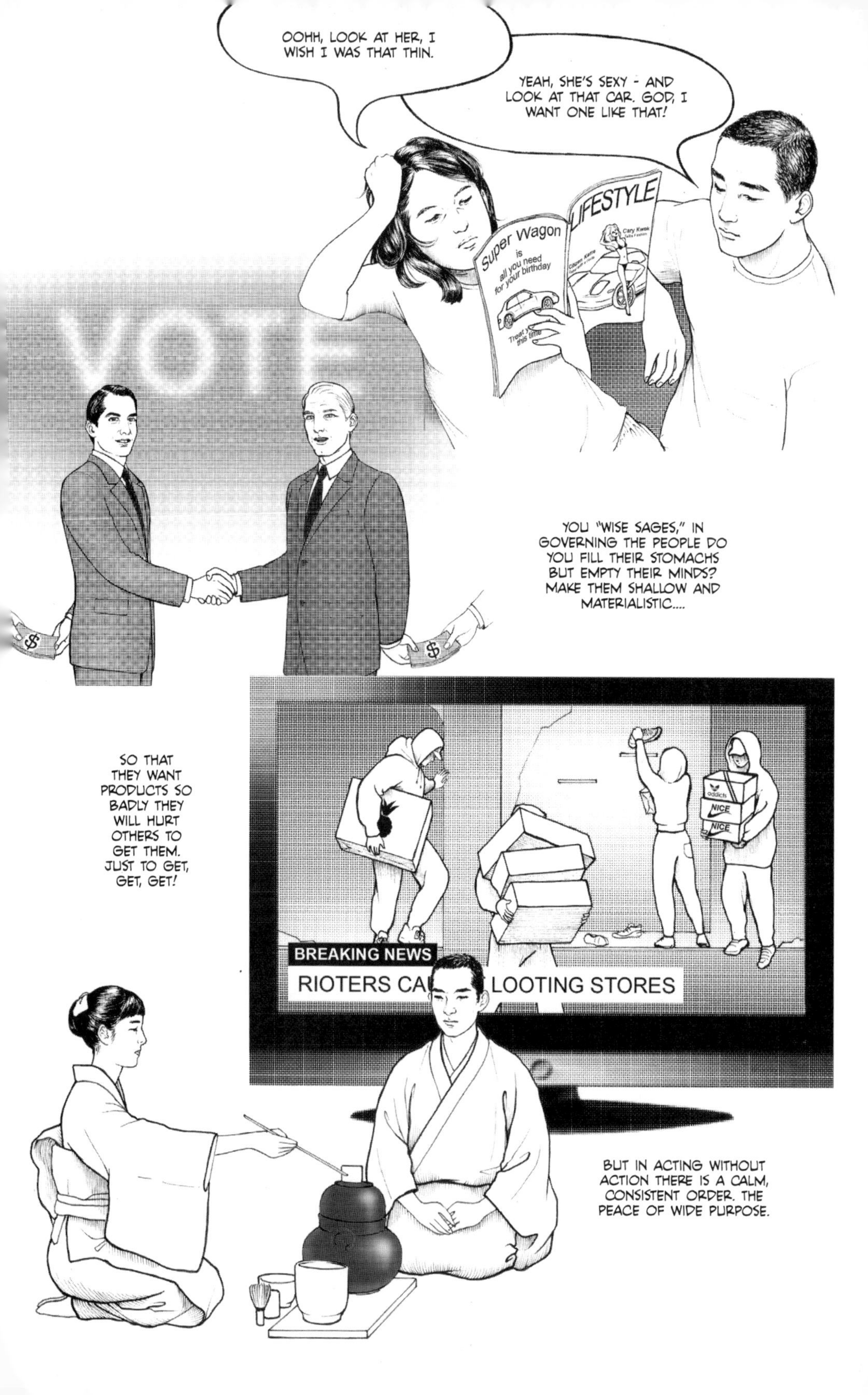
OOHH, LOOK AT HER, I WISH I WAS THAT THIN.
YEAH, SHE'S SEXY - AND LOOK AT THAT CAR. GOD, I WANT ONE LIKE THAT!
Super Wagon is all you need for your birthday
LIFESTYLE
VOTE
YOU "WISE SAGES," IN GOVERNING THE PEOPLE DO YOU FILL THEIR STOMACHS BUT EMPTY THEIR MINDS? MAKE THEM SHALLOW AND MATERIALISTIC....
SO THAT THEY WANT PRODUCTS SO BADLY THEY WILL HURT OTHERS TO GET THEM. JUST TO GET, GET, GET!
addicts
NICE
NICE
BREAKING NEWS
RIOTERS CA
LOOTING STORES
BUT IN ACTING WITHOUT ACTION THERE IS A CALM, CONSISTENT ORDER. THE PEACE OF WIDE PURPOSE.

# 4

The Way is as empty as an empty bowl,

Yet when used, it never fills.

Deep and ill-defined, it resembles the distant ancestor
of all things.

It blunts sharp edges, unravels their tangles,

softens their blazing light,

and blends one with their dust.

Gentle and overflowing, it always seems to be there.

I don't know who gives it birth;

It appears to precede the creator of us all.

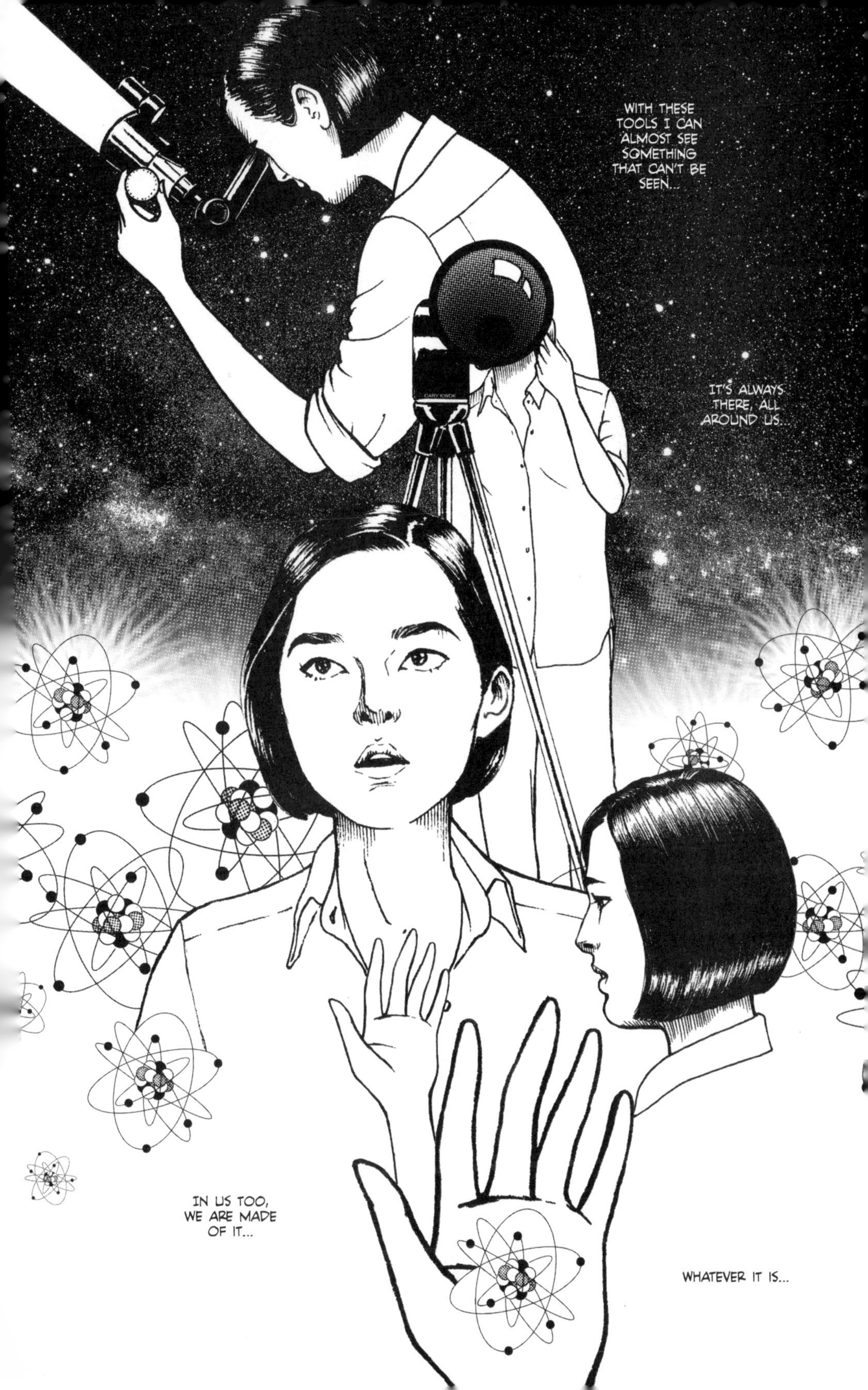
WITH THESE TOOLS I CAN ALMOST SEE SOMETHING THAT CAN'T BE SEEN...
IT'S ALWAYS THERE, ALL AROUND US...
IN US TOO, WE ARE MADE OF IT...
WHATEVER IT IS...

# 5

Heaven and Earth are not out to make friends;

Thus, they treat all creatures as straw dogs.

The sage is not out to make friends;

Thus, he treats the people as straw dogs.

Perhaps this is something like a bellows between Heaven and Earth:

It is empty, but never exhausted;

It moves, and creatures are manifested endlessly.

A lot of words will get you nowhere;

Better just to stay centered.

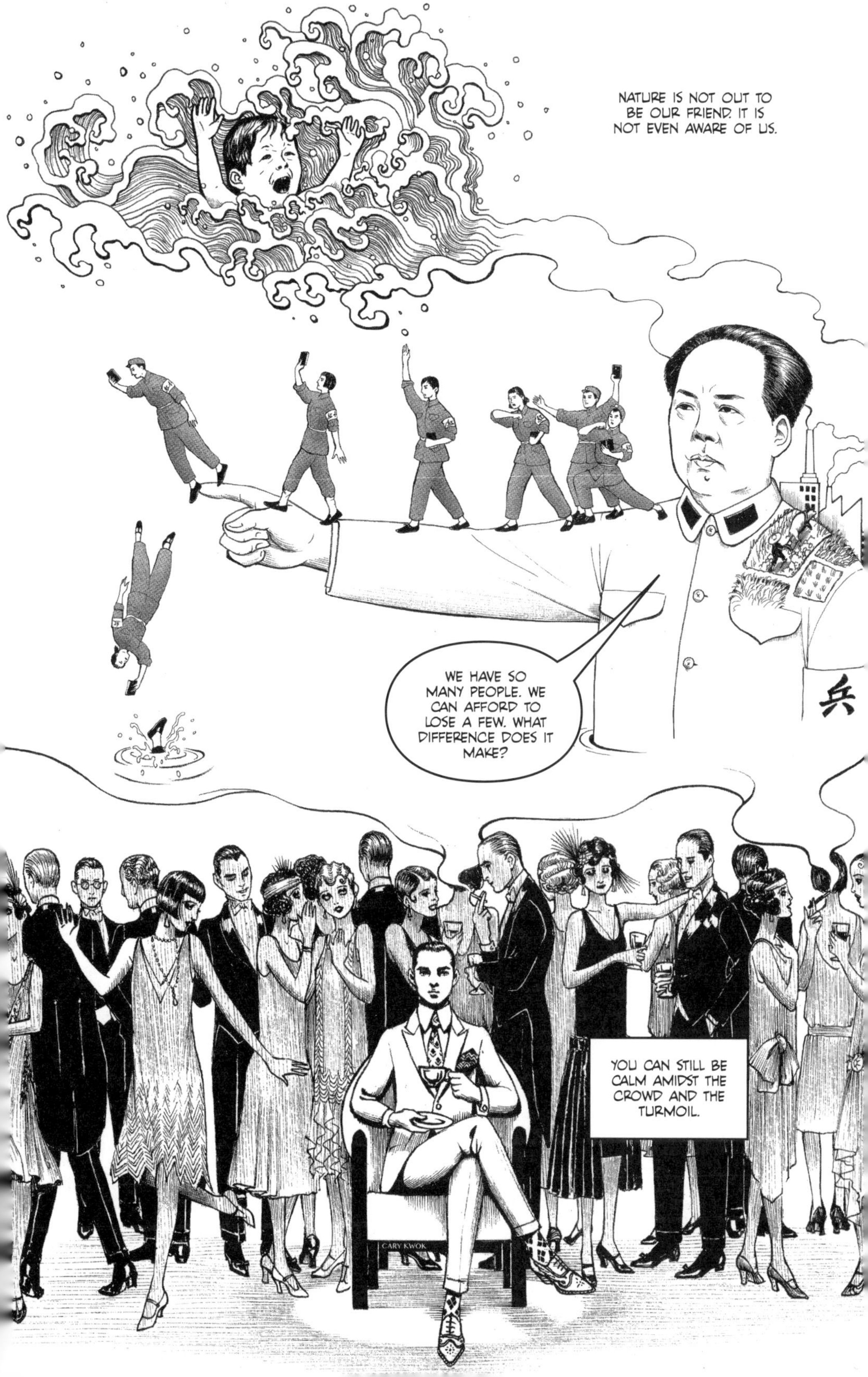
NATURE IS NOT OUT TO BE OUR FRIEND. IT IS NOT EVEN AWARE OF US.
WE HAVE SO MANY PEOPLE. WE CAN AFFORD TO LOSE A FEW. WHAT DIFFERENCE DOES IT MAKE?
兵
YOU CAN STILL BE CALM AMIDST THE CROWD AND THE TURMOIL.
CARY KWOK

# 6

The daemon of the valley does not die;

It is called the dark and mysterious female.

The gate of the dark and mysterious female

Is called the root of Heaven and Earth.

It seems to exist like an unending thread;

Use it—it never wears out.

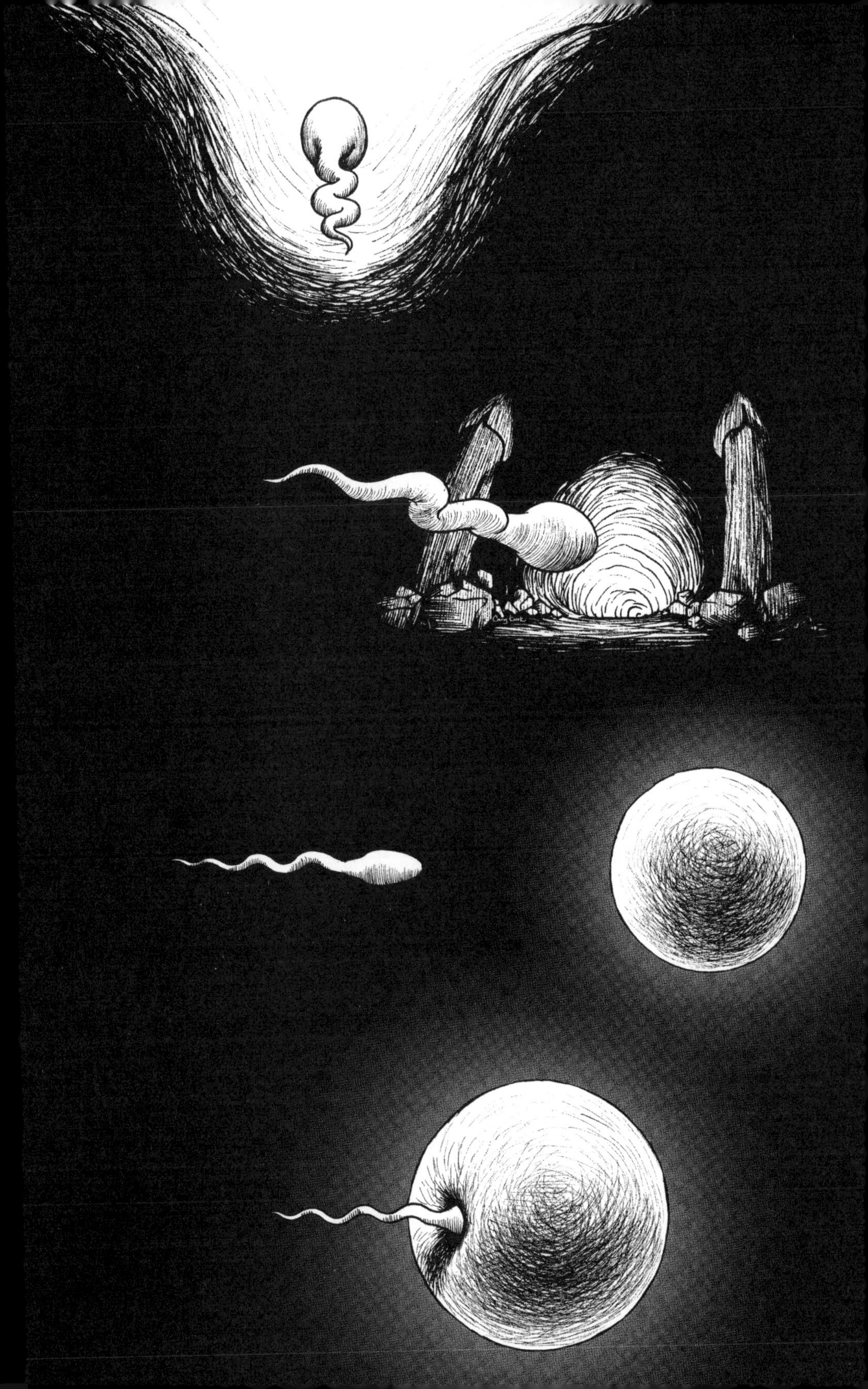

# 7

Heaven is everlasting; Earth, age-old.

The reason Heaven and Earth are everlasting and age-old:

They do not live for themselves.

Thus, they are able to endure.

Therefore the sage

>Puts himself last, but remains at the fore;

>Puts himself outside, but stays within.

Is it not due to his selflessness,

That he himself is fulfilled?

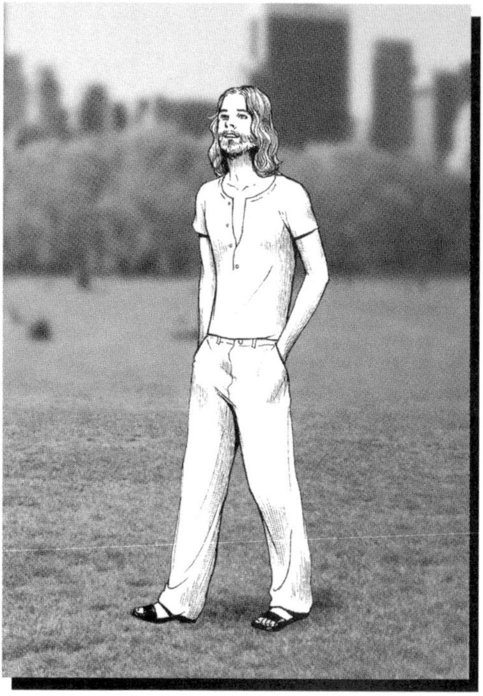
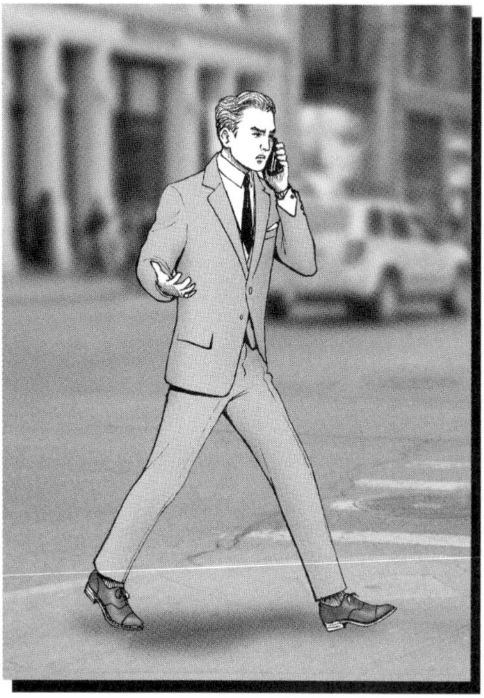
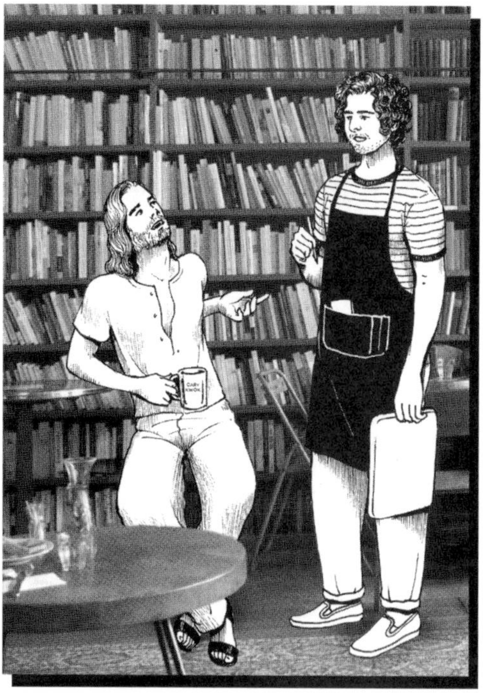
CARY KWOK
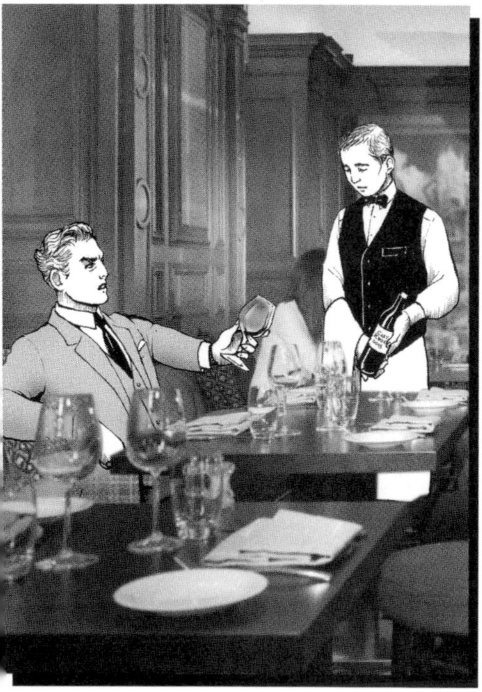

# 8

The greatest good is like water.

Water's virtue is that it benefits all creatures,

but contends with none;

It resides in places most men hate.

Thus, it takes after the Way.

For a place to live, the land itself is considered good;

For the mind, depth is considered good;

For society, sympathy is considered good;

For speaking, standing by one's words is considered good;

For governance, managing the flow is considered good;

For actual events, ability is considered good;

For movement, the right timing is considered good.

So listen: only in noncontention is there no blame.

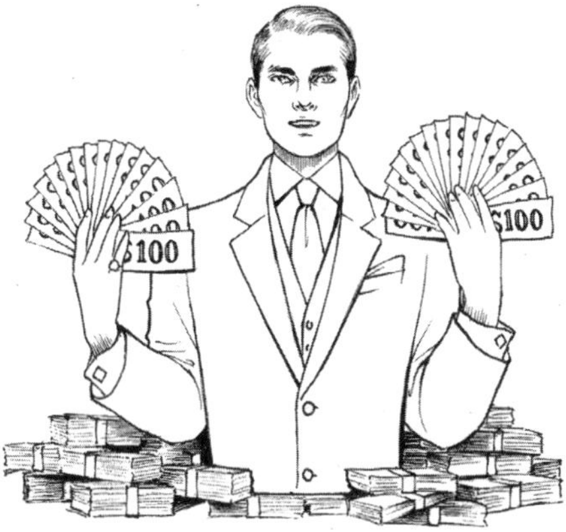
$100
$100

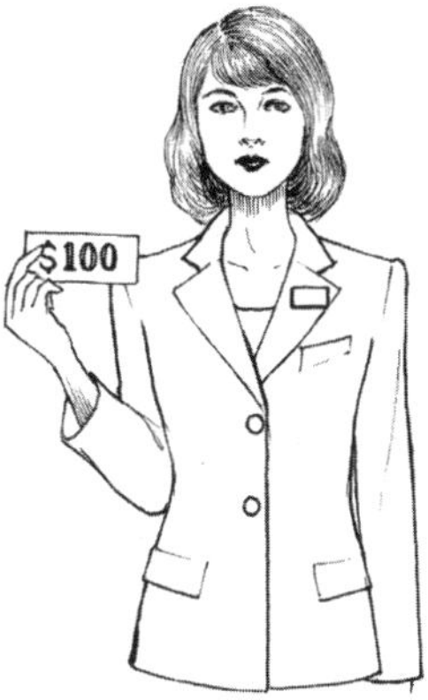
$100

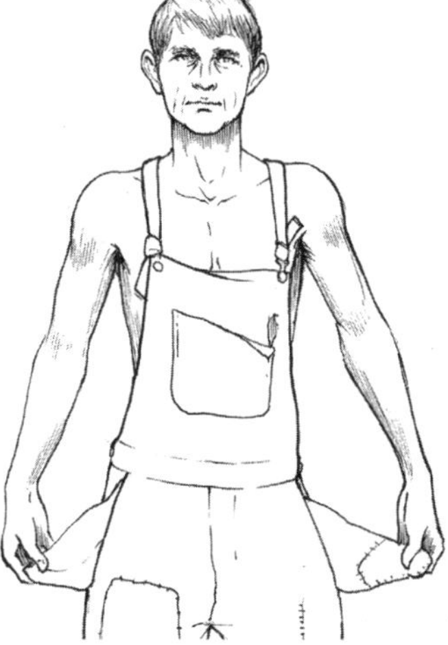

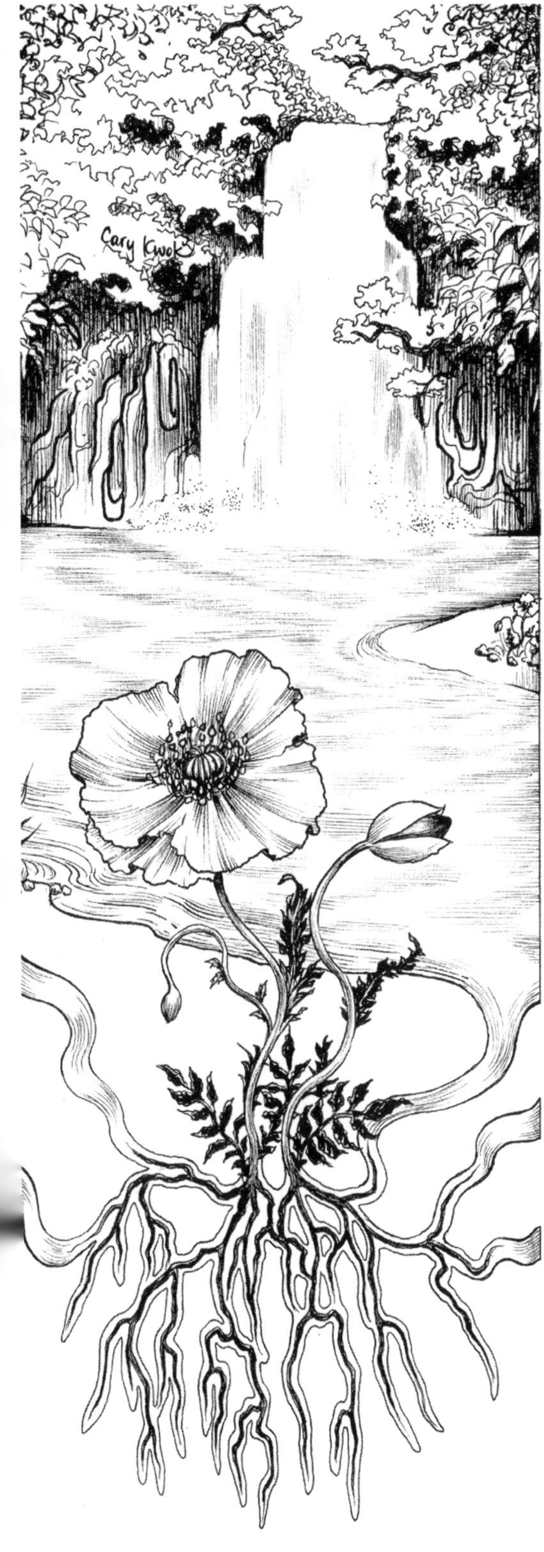
Cary Kwok

# 9

Better than holding the cup until filled to the brim,

Is knowing when to stop.

If you continue to temper and sharpen a blade,

It will not hold its edge for long.

When gold and jewels fill the hall,

Keeping them under *your* roof will be difficult.

Riding the high horse of your own wealth and position,

You will invite censure all on your own.

When you have completed some meritorious deed,

Back out and go home.

This is heaven's Way.

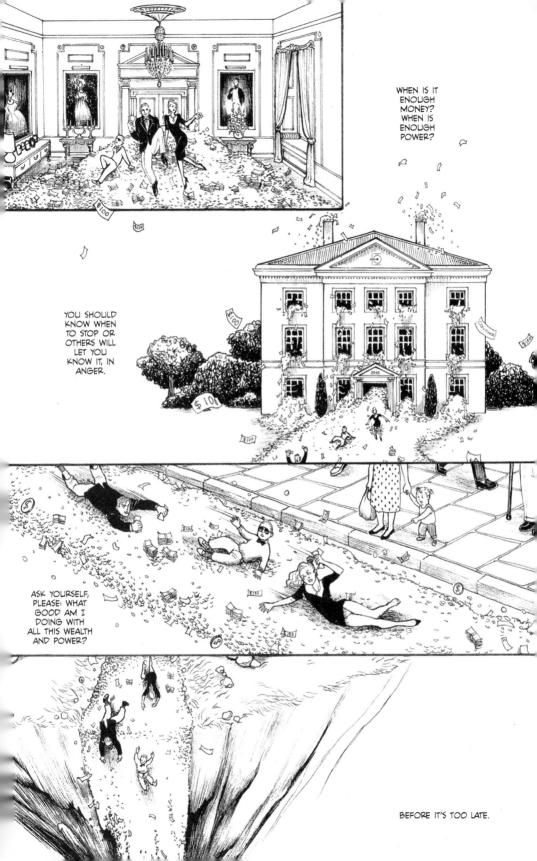

WHEN IS IT ENOUGH MONEY? WHEN IS ENOUGH POWER?

YOU SHOULD KNOW WHEN TO STOP OR OTHERS WILL LET YOU KNOW IT, IN ANGER.

ASK YOURSELF, PLEASE: WHAT GOOD AM I DOING WITH ALL THIS WEALTH AND POWER?

BEFORE IT'S TOO LATE.

# 10

Riding the wild corporeal spirit *and* embracing the One:

Can you do this without letting one of them go?

Concentrating your *ch'i and* mastering the pliant:

Can you do this and become like a nursing child?

Cleaning off the stains from the mirror of your mind:

Can you do this without streaking it yourself?

Loving the people *and* steering the country:

Can you do this without fabrication?

Opening and closing the Gate of heaven:

Can you do this acting as the female?

Sending out a bright and clear wisdom in all directions:

Can you do this unconsciously?

Bring things to life and nurture them,

But have no thoughts of possession.

Act without relying on anything;

Bring things along, but do not take charge.

This is the dark and mysterious virtue.

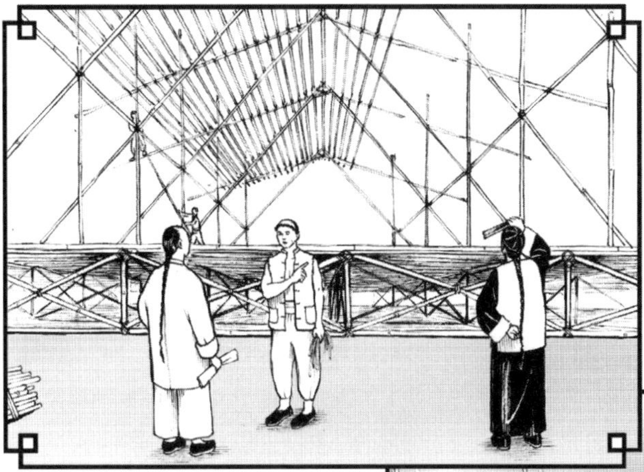

THE POWERFUL SHOULD ACT AS IF THEY HAD NO POWER.

ASK, RATHER THAN ORDER; GUIDE RATHER THAN GOAD; FACILITATE, DON'T FORCE. ALLOW OTHERS TO CHOOSE AND TO THINK FOR THEMSELVES.

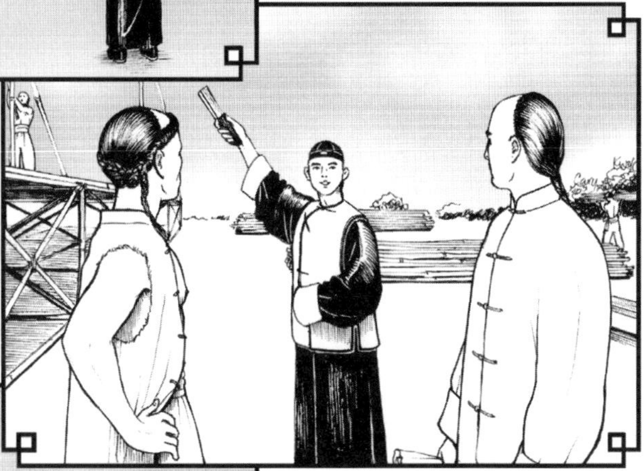

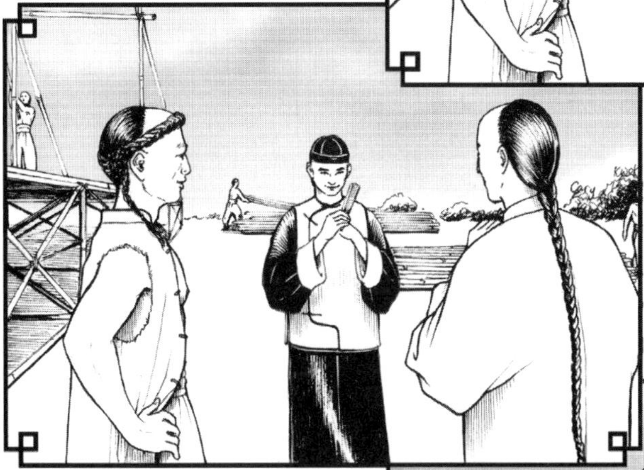

BE GENTLE WITH OTHERS ALONG THE WAY. THEY ARE NOT MEANS TO AN END; THEY ARE THE WAY ITSELF.

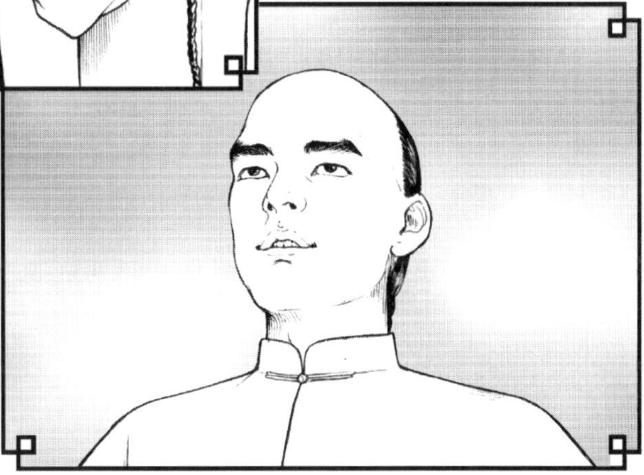

# 11

Thirty spokes make the nave of a wheel,

Yet it is the nonbeing at the center of the wheel that is the wheel's utility.

It is the kneaded clay that fashions a pot,

Yet it is the nonexistence inside the pot that is the pot's utility.

It is the chiseling out of windows and a door that make a room,

Yet it is the nonexistence in the door and windows that is the room's utility.

Therefore, it is by existence that we set the stage,

But by nonexistence that we have utility.

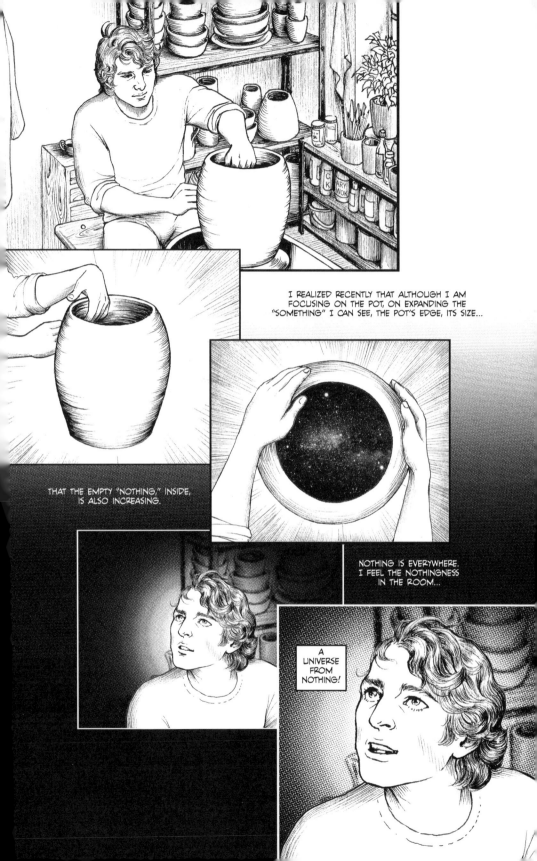

I REALIZED RECENTLY THAT ALTHOUGH I AM FOCUSING ON THE POT, ON EXPANDING THE "SOMETHING" I CAN SEE, THE POT'S EDGE, ITS SIZE...

THAT THE EMPTY "NOTHING," INSIDE, IS ALSO INCREASING.

NOTHING IS EVERYWHERE. I FEEL THE NOTHINGNESS IN THE ROOM...

A UNIVERSE FROM NOTHING!

# 12

The five colors combined will make you blind.

The five sounds combined will make you deaf.

The five tastes combined will confuse your mouth.

Whipping your horse around hunting in the fields will make you as crazy as a mad dog.

Valuables hard to obtain will hobble your behavior.

For this reason, the sage thinks about his stomach, but not about what he sees around him.

He takes the one, but passes the other by.

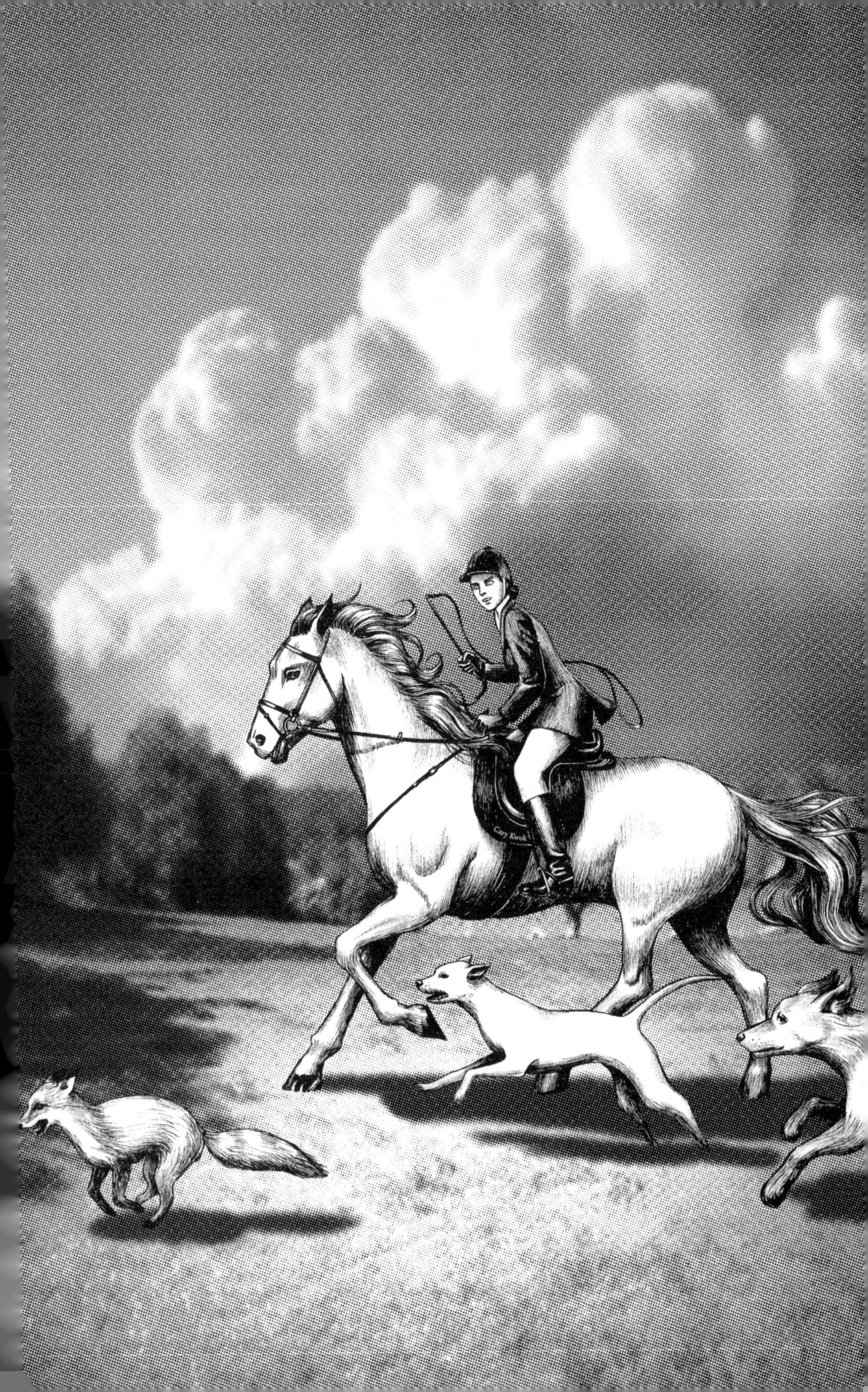
Cary Kwok

# 13

Be alarmed by either honors or disgrace.

Respect those things that pain the mind as you would those that pain the body.

What does it mean to say that you should be alarmed by either honors or disgrace?

Consider honors to be of a lower order:

Be alarmed by receiving them;

Be alarmed by losing them.

This is what it means to say that you should be alarmed by either honors or disgrace.

What does it mean to say that you should respect those things that pain the mind as you would those that pain the body?

The reason that you have things that pain the mind is because you have a physical body.

If you did not have a physical body, how would you have things that pain the mind?

Thus, a person who respects his body *and* rules an empire

May indeed be entrusted with the empire;

A person who loves his body and rules the empire

May indeed be depended upon to rule.

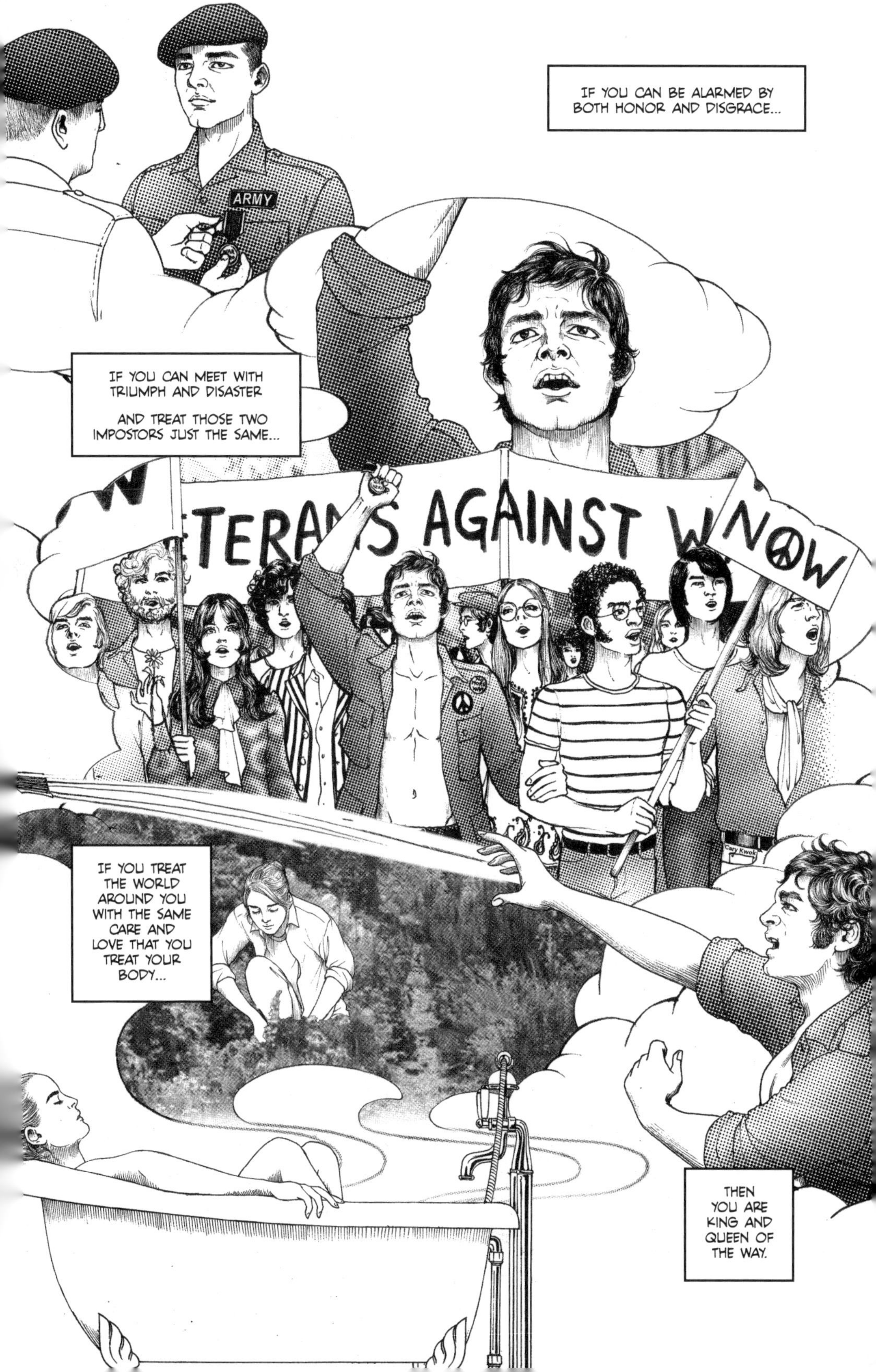
IF YOU CAN BE ALARMED BY BOTH HONOR AND DISGRACE...
ARMY
IF YOU CAN MEET WITH TRIUMPH AND DISASTER
AND TREAT THOSE TWO IMPOSTORS JUST THE SAME...
ETERA S AGAINST W
NOW
Cary Kwok
IF YOU TREAT THE WORLD AROUND YOU WITH THE SAME CARE AND LOVE THAT YOU TREAT YOUR BODY...
THEN YOU ARE KING AND QUEEN OF THE WAY.

# 14

You stare at it fixedly, but do not see it.

It is called Dim.

You listen to it carefully, but do not hear it.

It is called Indistinct.

You touch it, but feel nothing.

It is called Vague.

These three cannot be investigated with clarity,

And mixed up like rushing water, act as one.

From above, it is not clear;

From below, it is not dark.

As continuous as an unending cord, it cannot be named,

And returns to No-Thing.

This is called the form of No-Form,

Or the shape of No-Thing.

It is called vacant and abstracted.

When you approach it, you will not see its head;

When you follow it, you will not see its behind.

Take tight grasp of the Way of antiquity

And you will lead present existence as you would a horse.

Being able to understand the Ancient Beginning with all of your senses,

Is called the beginning thread of the Way.

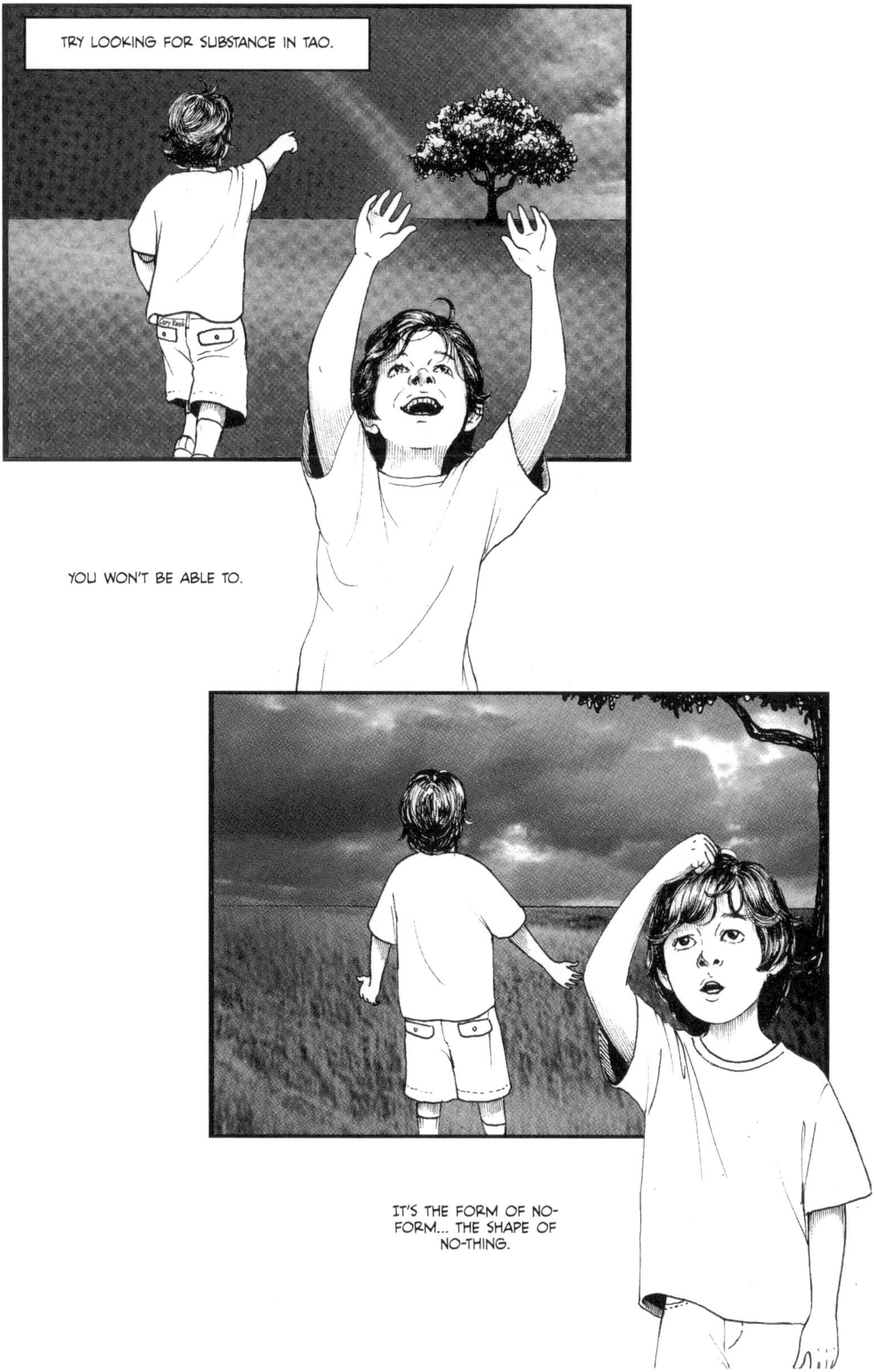
TRY LOOKING FOR SUBSTANCE IN TAO.
YOU WON'T BE ABLE TO.
IT'S THE FORM OF NO-FORM... THE SHAPE OF NO-THING.

# 15

The men who practiced the Way effectively in the past

Were unfathomable and beyond description;

You could not get a sense of their depth

And although you could not get a sense of their depth,

I will persist, and try to create a picture of them:

> Hesitating, like crossing a stream in winter;
>
> Wavering, like fearing demons with clubs on all sides;
>
> Respectful, like being a guest;
>
> Pliant, like ice about to melt;
>
> Unpretentious, like rough lumber;
>
> In plain view, like a valley;
>
> Mixing and mingling, like muddy water.

Who can gradually clarify muddy water with tranquility?

Who can gradually bring life into the complacent with activity?

Those who care for the Way as they would a child carried on their back.

Do not wish to be filled to the brim.

Exactly because they are not filled to the brim,

When worn out like old clothing, they are renewed yet again.

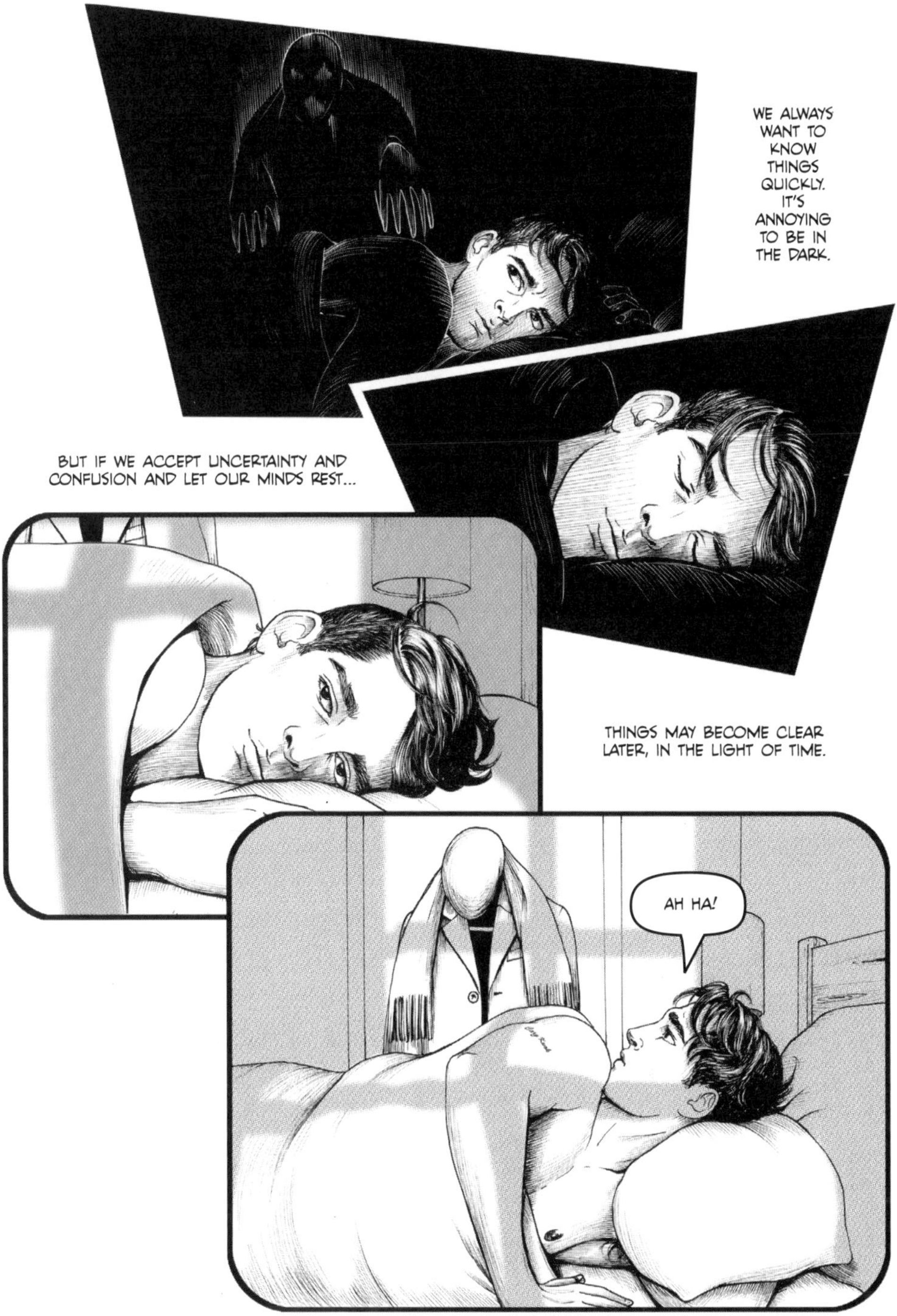
WE ALWAYS WANT TO KNOW THINGS QUICKLY. IT'S ANNOYING TO BE IN THE DARK.
BUT IF WE ACCEPT UNCERTAINTY AND CONFUSION AND LET OUR MINDS REST...
THINGS MAY BECOME CLEAR LATER, IN THE LIGHT OF TIME.
AH HA!

# 16

Bring yourself steadily to absolute emptiness.

Preserve your tranquility in a careful fashion, like a slowly walking horse.

All creatures are brought into being one after another,

But with this, I perceive their return.

Listen, creatures are of countless varieties,

But each returns to its root.

Returning to its root is called tranquility,

And this is called returning to its naturally given course.

Returning to its naturally given course is called the Unchanging;

Understanding the Unchanging is called the bright and clear.

If you do not understand the Unchanging,

You will be doing things in the dark, and this is ill-omened.

If you know the Unchanging, you will have latitude;

Having latitude is being open to all.

Being open to all is being kingly;

Being kingly is being as broad as heaven.

Being as broad as heaven is the Way,

And the Way transcends time.

In this way, you will be without danger until your body sinks beneath the sea of existence.

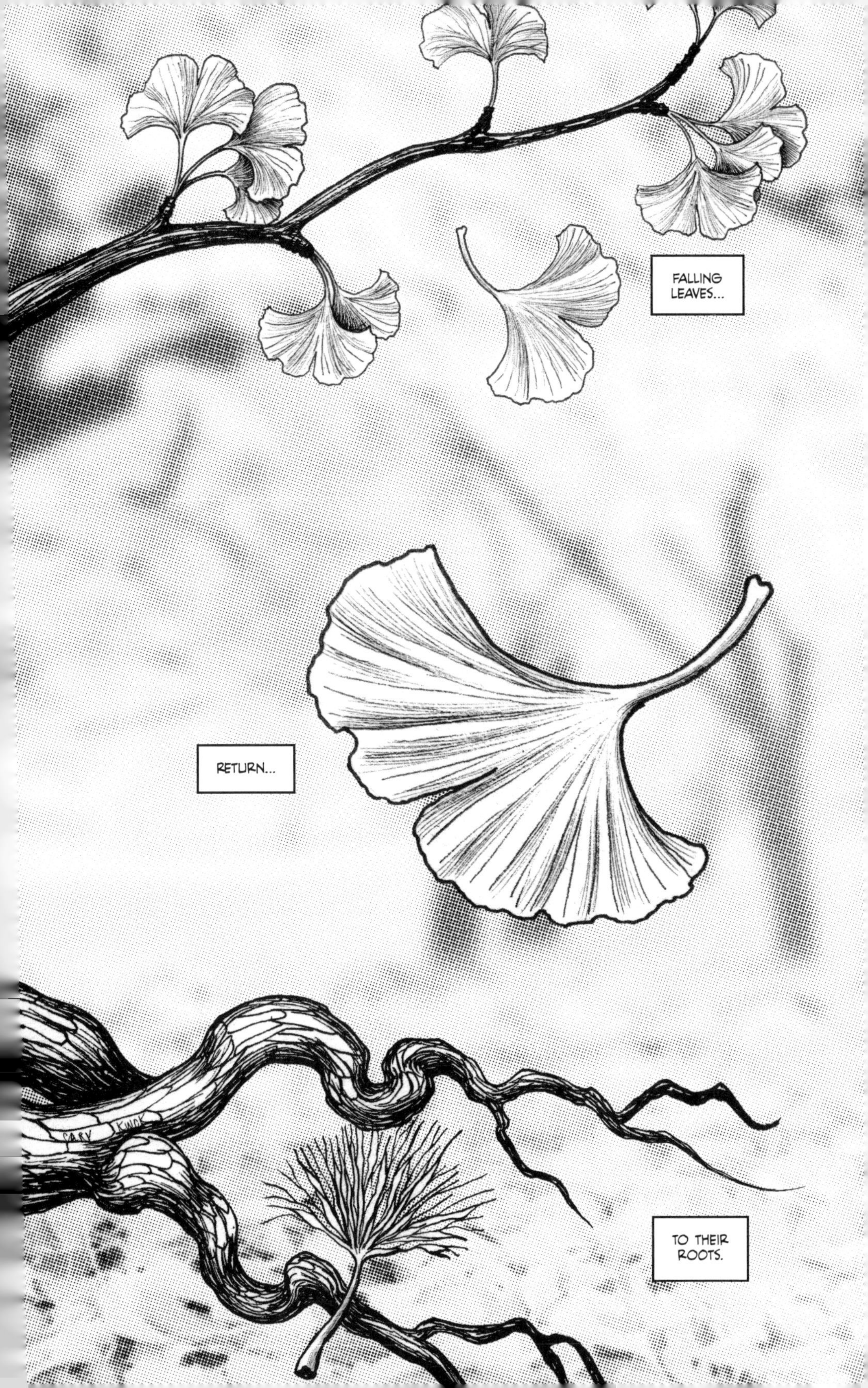
FALLING LEAVES...
RETURN...
TO THEIR ROOTS.

# 17

The greatest superior is he whose inferiors know only that he is there.

The next in line is he who is held in familial affection and praised.

The next is he who is feared as a demon armed with cudgels.

The lowest is he who is regarded as a lightweight.

When a man does not sufficiently stand by his words, there will be no standing by words anywhere.

Think broadly and value your words as wealth.

Finish your work, accomplish what you set your hand to, and the people will call you a natural.

THE GREATEST LEADERS/ TEACHERS/ PARENTS ARE THOSE WHOSE POWER IS HARDLY FELT AT ALL.

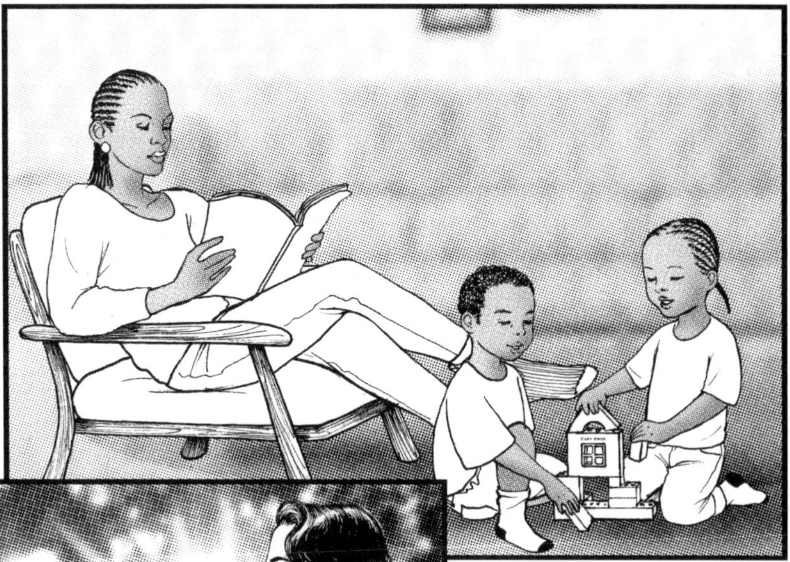

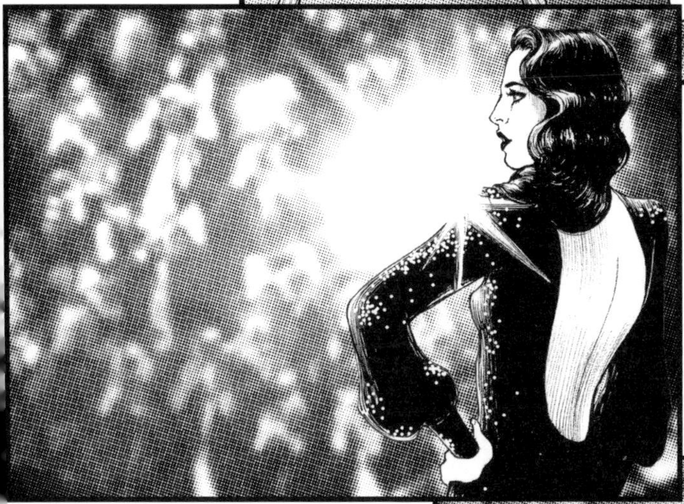

NEXT DOWN ARE THOSE OSTENTATIOUSLY LOVED AND PRAISED.

NEXT DOWN ARE THOSE WHO ARE FEARED.

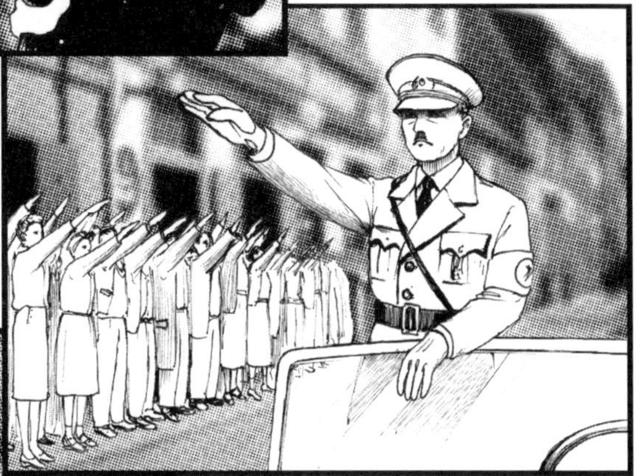

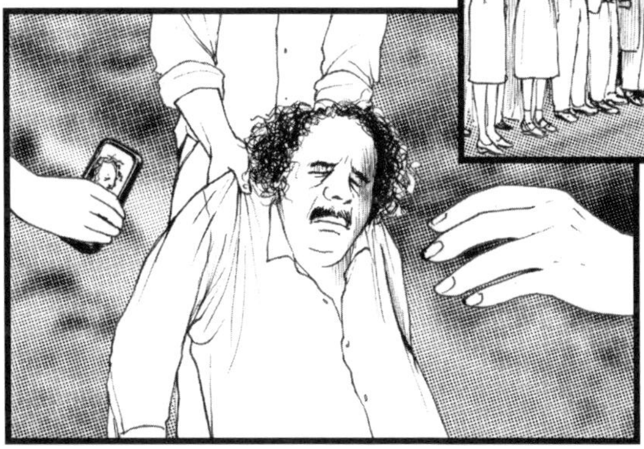

THE LOWEST DOWN ARE BRUSHED ASIDE.

# 18

When the Great Way is abandoned, conscious sympathy and "correct" behavior will be at hand.

When masters of wisdom and quick wit appear, great hypocrisy will be at hand.

When the six family relationships are not in harmony, filial piety and loving upbringing will be at hand.

When the state is in confusion and its vision is dim, "sincere and loyal" retainers will be at hand.

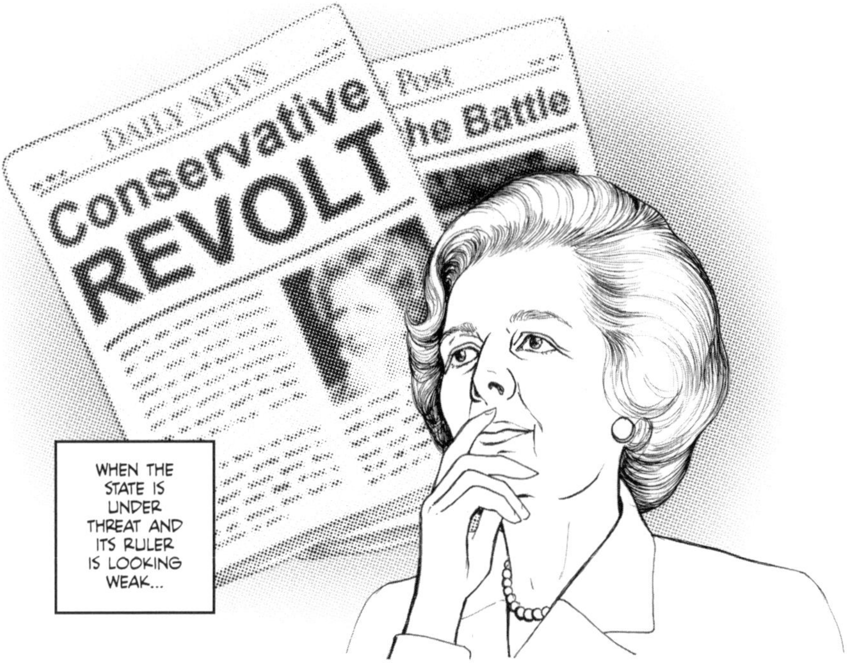
DAILY NEWS
Conservative REVOLT
Post
he Battle
WHEN THE STATE IS UNDER THREAT AND ITS RULER IS LOOKING WEAK...

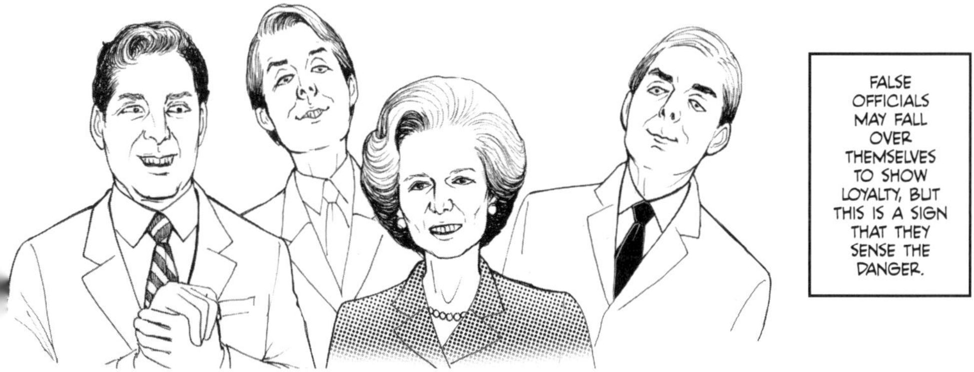
FALSE OFFICIALS MAY FALL OVER THEMSELVES TO SHOW LOYALTY, BUT THIS IS A SIGN THAT THEY SENSE THE DANGER.

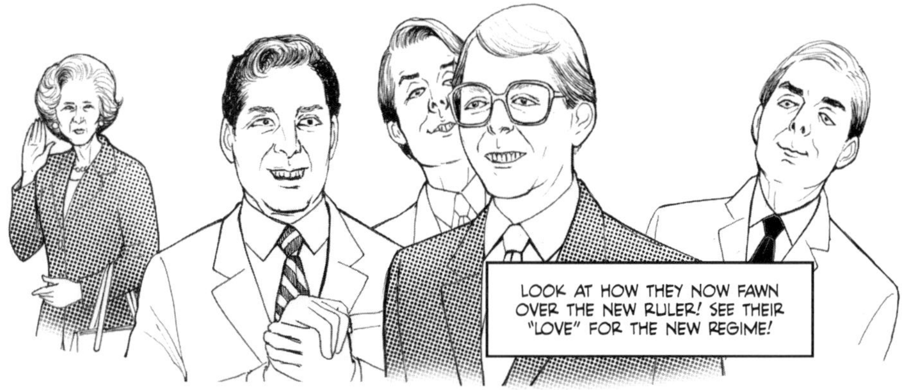
LOOK AT HOW THEY NOW FAWN OVER THE NEW RULER! SEE THEIR "LOVE" FOR THE NEW REGIME!

# 19

Cut off saintliness as a knife would cut a thread, throw away wisdom as you would dust from a dustpan,

And the people's preparedness for life will increase a hundredfold.

Cut off human-heartedness and throw away ornamental conduct,

And the people will do a direct turnaround to filial piety and a nurturing heart.

Cut off ingeniousness and throw away gain,

And burglars and armed bandits will not be at hand.

These three considered simply as general patterns will be insufficient.

Therefore I must attach something concrete to hold on to:

> Visibly demonstrate a simplicity as unadorned as white thread, and embrace a candidness as plain as bark.

> Make less of yourself and reduce greed.

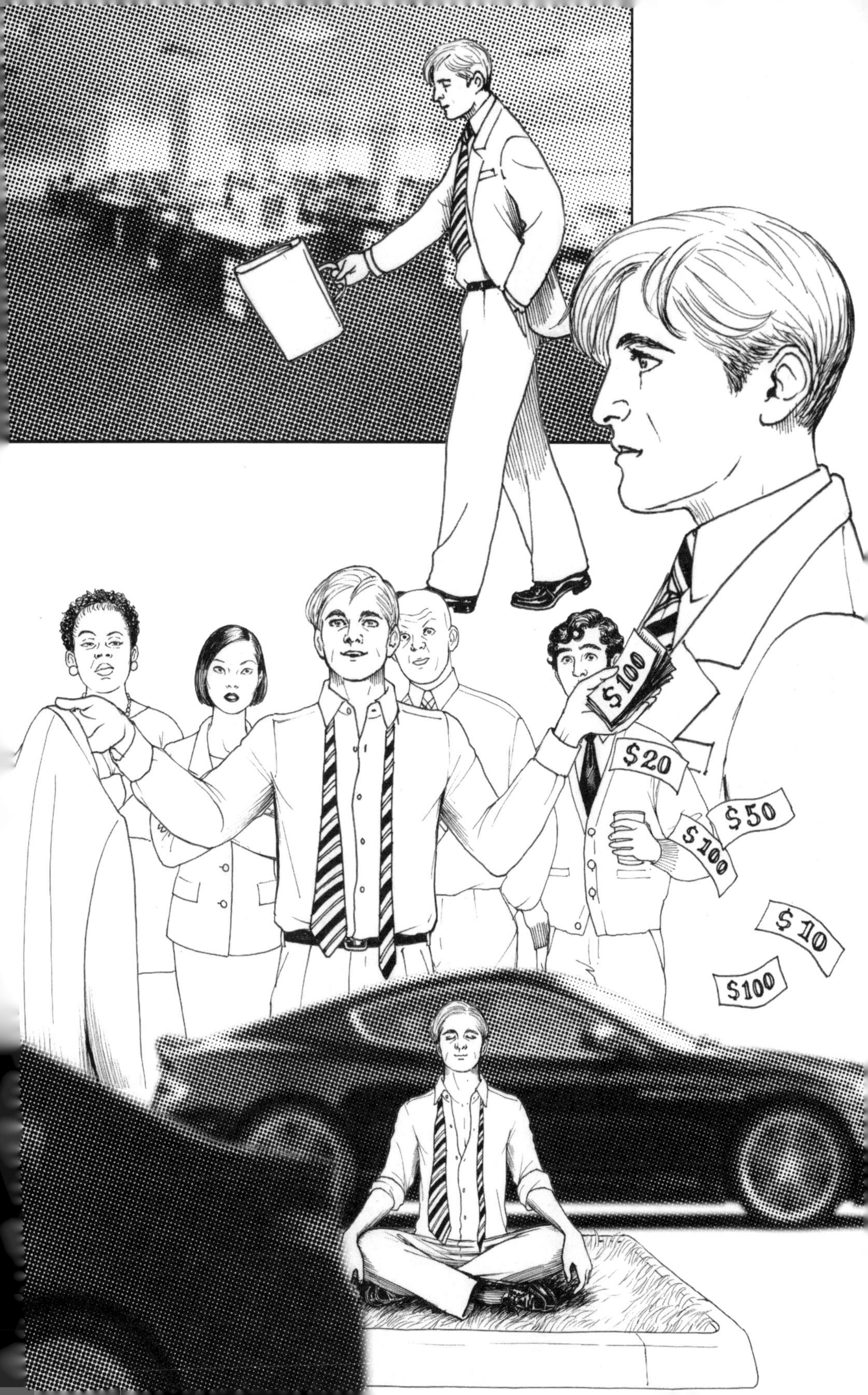
$100
$20
$50
$100
$10
$100

# 20

Leave off studying with your head in your hands, and you will not be obsessed about what to do next.

How much divergence is there between "Yes, sir!" and "As you please"?

How much divergence between the attractive and the not so attractive?

It's not that you should not fear what other people dread;

But it's all as entangled as a thicket and, sadly, you'll never get even halfway through.

The majority of people are bright and pleased:

> As though guests at a great feast,

> As though climbing up a high platform from which to look out in spring.

I alone am moored like a boat, with no portents of moving on;

Like a suckling child who has not yet smiled.

Loaded down and tired, it seems that I have no place to go home.

The majority of people all have more than enough under their roofs,

While I alone seem to have forgotten all my goods along the way.

Do I, alas, have the mind of a fool?


Ahh, undiscriminating and in the dark,

While the average man is sunshine bright.

I alone am as dim as dusk,

While the average man sees everything in detail.

I alone have a fenced-in mind,

Like a shallow and irresolute sea,

Like a high-pitched wind that never stops.

The common run of men all have something to do,

But I alone am disordered and indiscriminate, resembling a hayseed from out of town.

I alone am unlike others,

And value being nourished at the Mother's breast.

# 21

The manifested forms contained within the Great
Virtue only follow along behind the Way.

That which is considered the real existence of the Way
is now abstract, now dim.

Now dim, now abstract: within it is form.

Now abstract, now dim: within it real existence is at
hand.

Darkly cavernous and like a moonless night: within it is
the quintessence.

This quintessence is the extreme truth: within it is the
stamp of proof.

From ancient times until the recent, it identifies itself
without fail,

And thus we examine the beginnings of all things.

How do I know this matter of the beginnings of all
things?

It's right here.

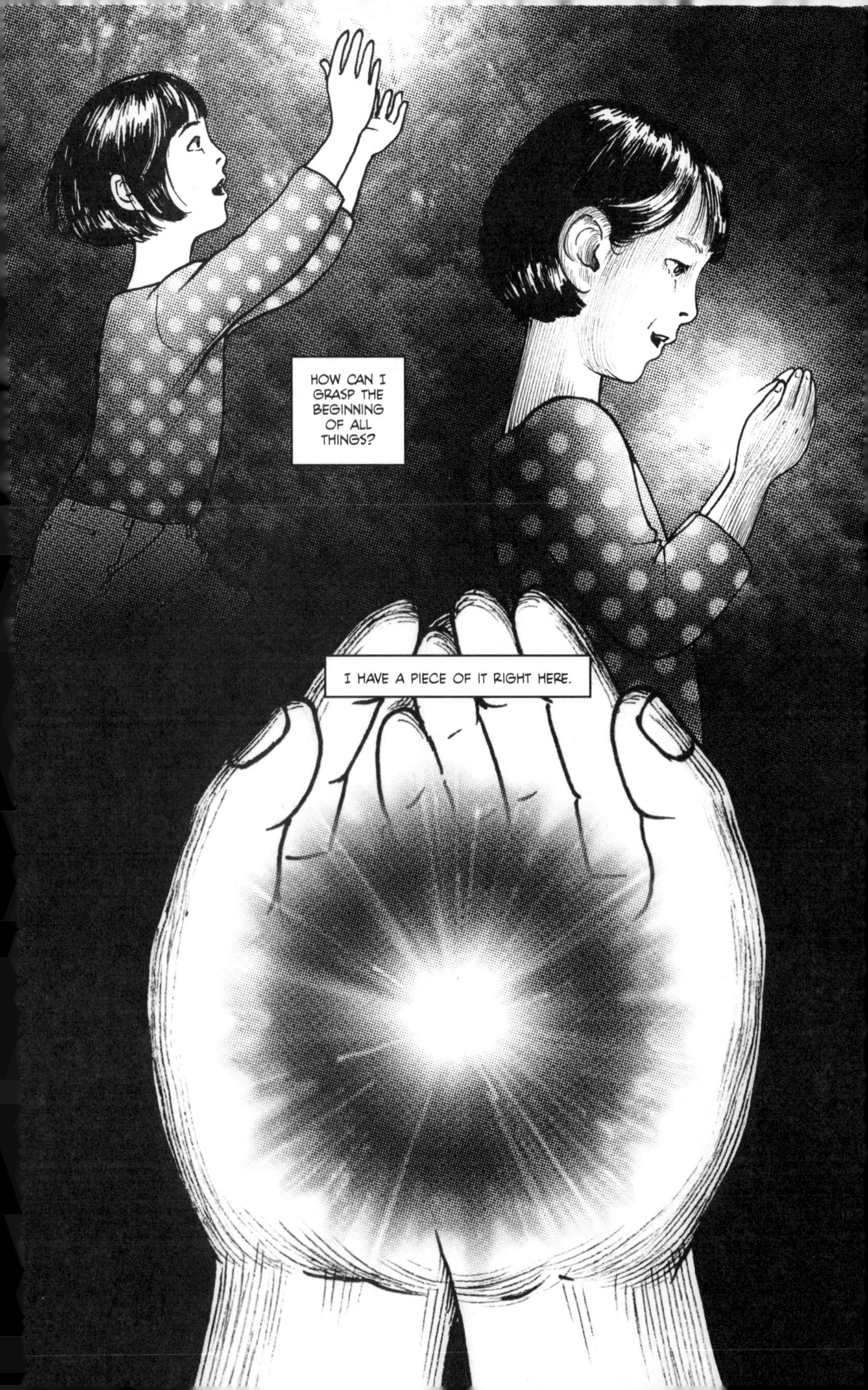
HOW CAN I GRASP THE BEGINNING OF ALL THINGS?
I HAVE A PIECE OF IT RIGHT HERE.

# 22

That which is twisted will remain whole.

That which bends will become straight.

That which is hollowed out like a melon will be filled to the brim.

That which is torn like cloth will be re-cut and made anew.

Having less, you can receive;

Having more, you become confused.


Therefore, the wise man

   Embraces the One, and becomes the model for all under heaven;

   Does not make himself seen, and therefore is as bright as the sun and moon;

   Does not consider himself good, and therefore is a pattern for all;

   Does not denigrate others to make himself look good, and therefore gets the credit;

   Does not make himself like the arrogant grip of a spear, and therefore becomes a staff of support.


Listen, it is simply that he does not contend.

Thus no one under heaven can contend with him.

The saying of the ancients, "The twisted will remain whole"–

How could these be empty words?

In truth, it will remain whole, and will return to the Source.

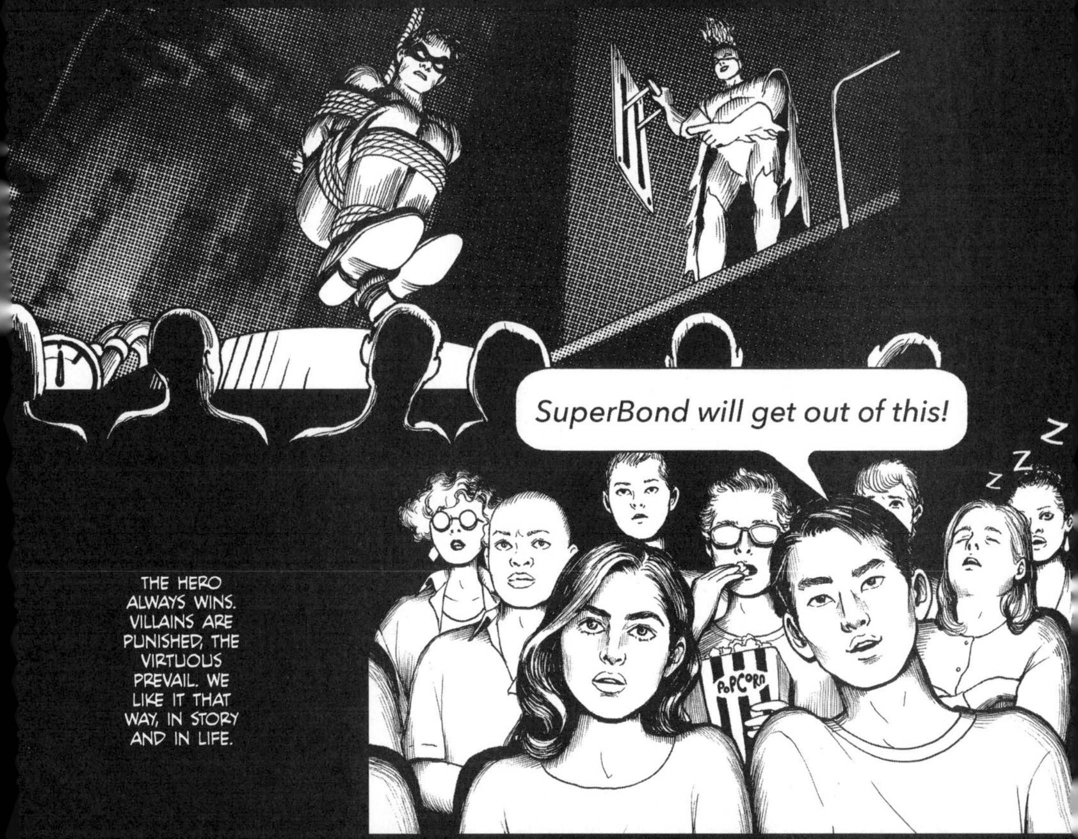
SuperBond will get out of this!
Z Z Z
THE HERO ALWAYS WINS. VILLAINS ARE PUNISHED, THE VIRTUOUS PREVAIL. WE LIKE IT THAT WAY, IN STORY AND IN LIFE.
POPCORN

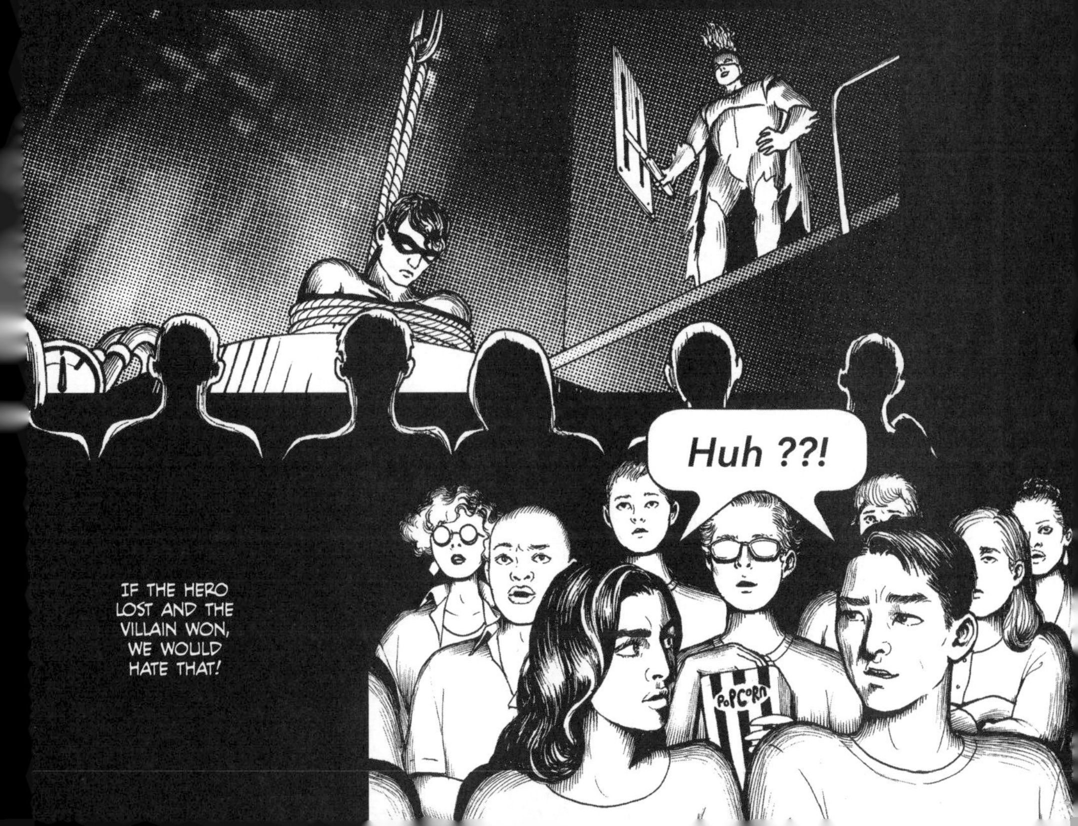
Huh ??!
IF THE HERO LOST AND THE VILLAIN WON, WE WOULD HATE THAT!
POPCORN

# 23

It is natural to have few words.

Thus, the whirlwind that blows things around as though they were bugs, does not last the morning.

Neither does the sudden storm last the day.

Who is it that concocts such things?

Heaven and Earth.

But Heaven and Earth cannot sustain them for long.

How, then, could Man?


Therefore, he who follows the Way in what he puts his hand to,

Will be included among the men of the Way

And will be included among men of virtue;

In losing the Way and its virtue, he will be included among those of similar loss.

Those who gather under the gate of the Way are in turn happily received by the Way.

Those who gather under the gate of virtue are in turn happily received by virtue.

Those who gather under the gate of loss are in turn happily received by loss.

When one does not sufficiently stand by his words,

A general loss of faith will be at hand.

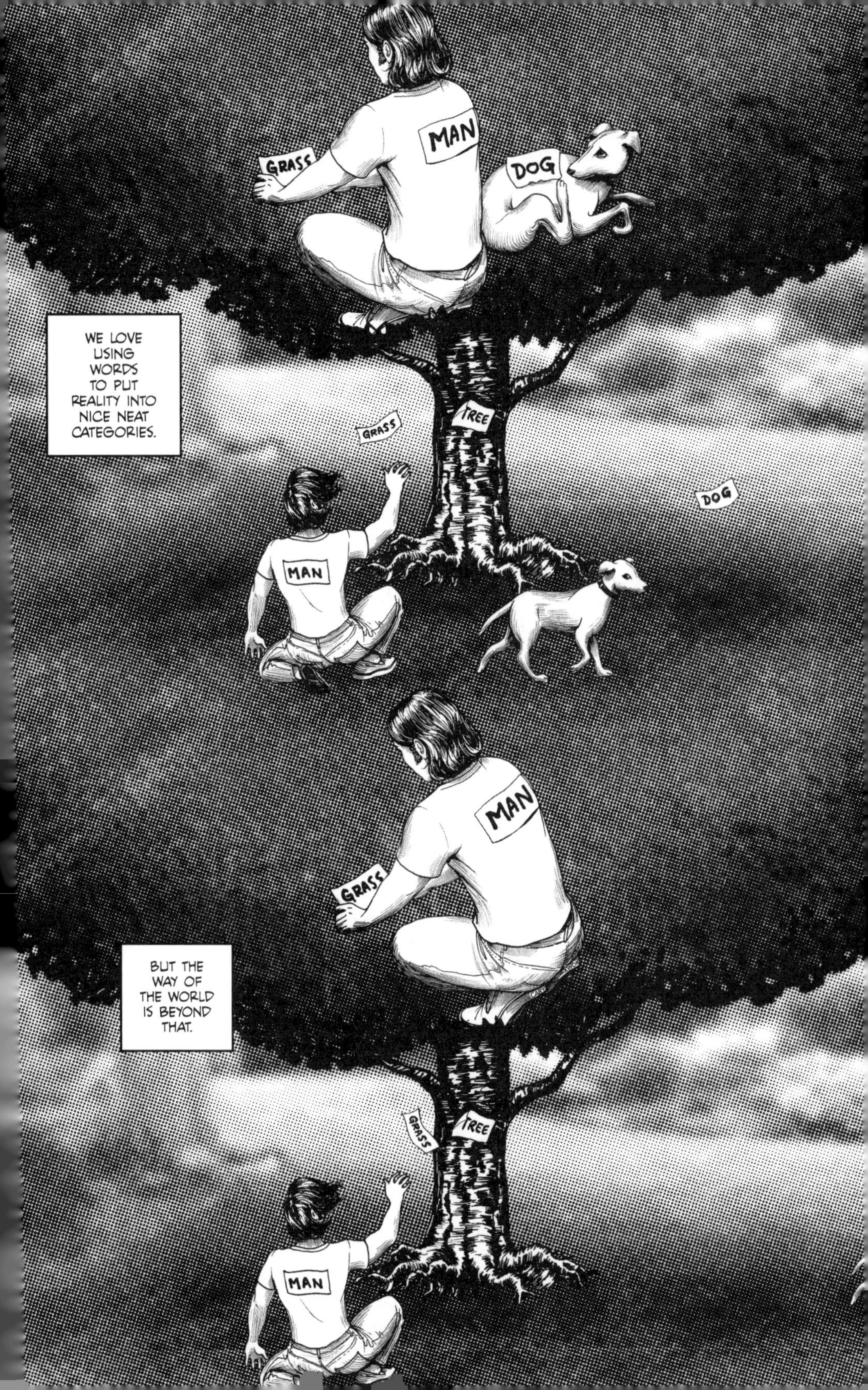
MAN
GRASS
DOG
WE LOVE USING WORDS TO PUT REALITY INTO NICE NEAT CATEGORIES.
TREE
GRASS
DOG
MAN
MAN
GRASS
BUT THE WAY OF THE WORLD IS BEYOND THAT.
GRASS
TREE
MAN

# 24

If you are up on tiptoes, you will not stand with confidence.

If you move along straddling the road, you will be unable to put one foot in front of the other.

If you make yourself seen, you will not be illustrious.

If you consider yourself right, you will not be taken as a model.

If you denigrate others, you will get no credit.

If you consider yourself the grip of a spear, you will never become a staff of support.


Those who abide in the Way

Call such things "leftover food" or "warts on your behavior."

Thus, those who possess the Way will be found elsewhere.

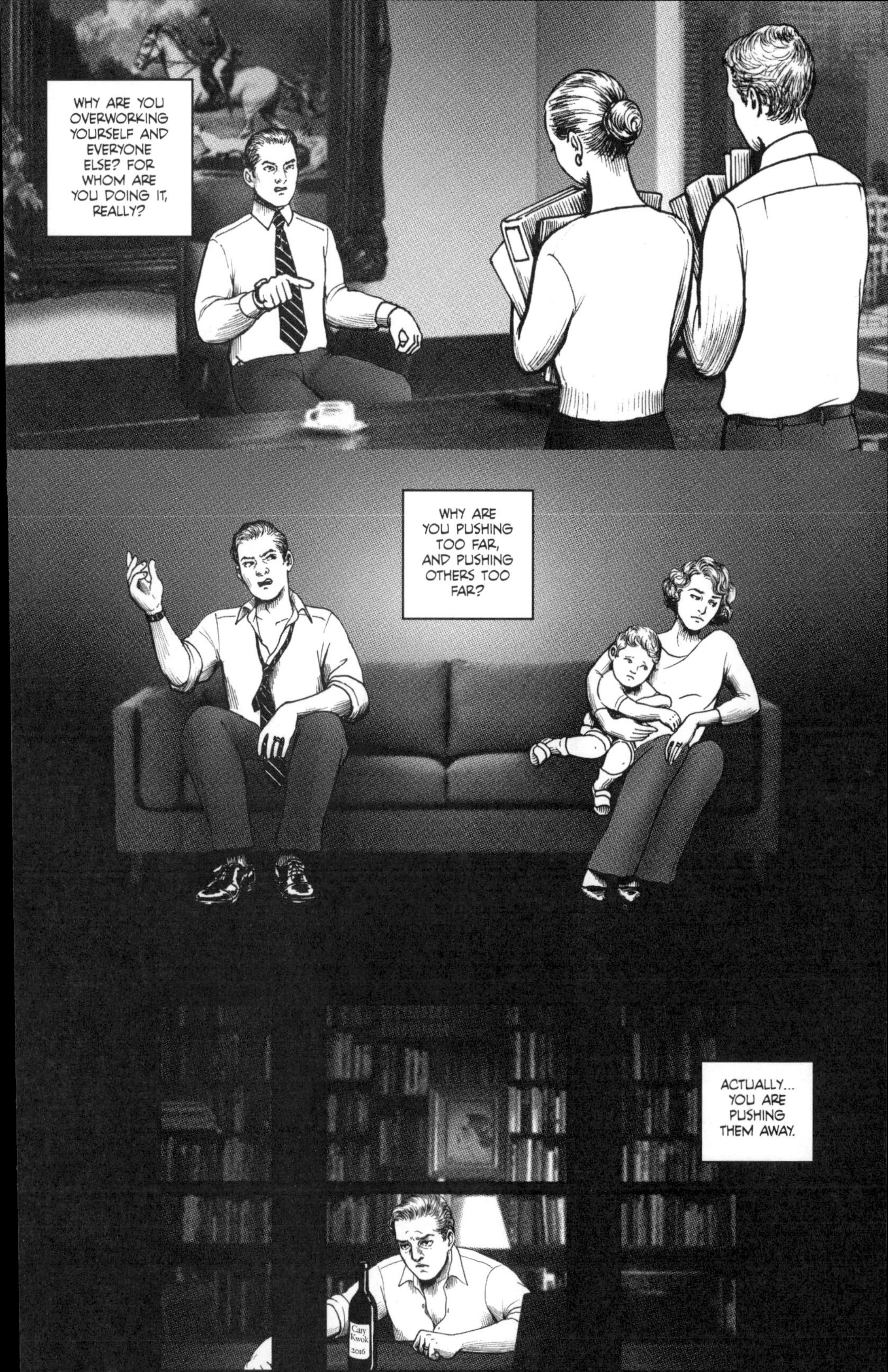
WHY ARE YOU OVERWORKING YOURSELF AND EVERYONE ELSE? FOR WHOM ARE YOU DOING IT, REALLY?
WHY ARE YOU PUSHING TOO FAR, AND PUSHING OTHERS TOO FAR?
ACTUALLY... YOU ARE PUSHING THEM AWAY.
Cary Kwok 2016

# 25

There is something mingled and ungraspable as bubbling water, and yet quite complete;

It exists before Heaven and Earth.

It is quiet and tranquil; empty and at rest.

It stands on its own, and cannot be altered;

Manifests itself in all things, and is never idle.

You could consider it the nursing mother of all under heaven.

I myself do not know its name, but for starters, call it the Way.

Pushed to make up a name, you could call it Great.

The Great is said to flow out and beyond;

Flowing out and beyond is said to journey far away;

To journey far away is said to return.


Thus, the Way is Great,

Heaven is Great,

Earth is Great,

And the king is also Great.

For all in existence, there are four Greats,

And the king takes his place as one of them.

Man follows the flow of the Earth.

Earth follows the flow of Heaven.

Heaven follows the flow of the Way.

The Way follows the flow of the Of-Itself-So.

WHERE DID EVERYTHING COME FROM? WHO OR WHAT CONCEIVED AND FRAMED US ALL?

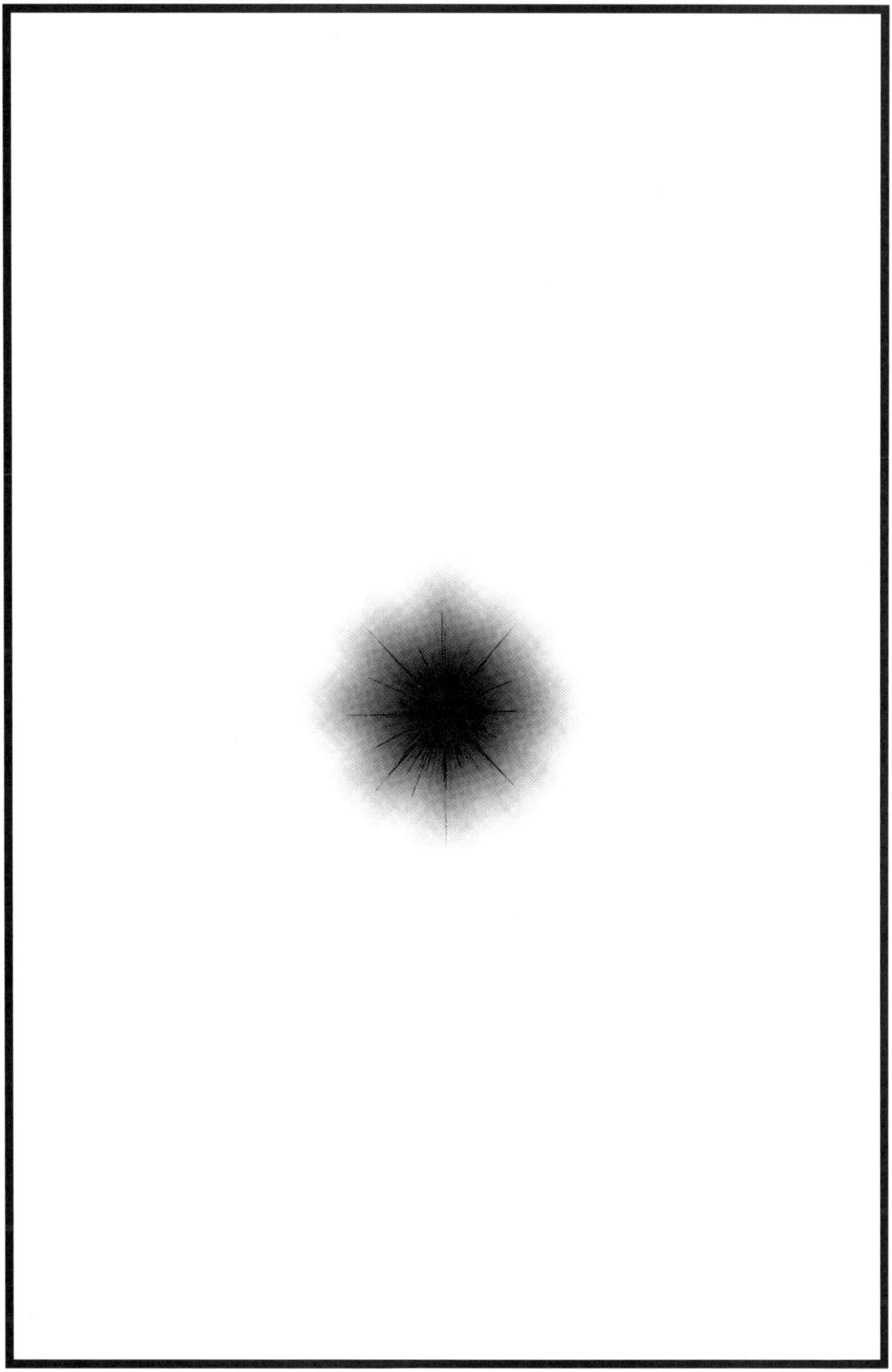

WHAT WAS THERE BEFORE THE BORDER LINES OF OUR WORLD WERE DRAWN?

# 26

The heavy fabricates the root of the light.

The tranquil fabricates command of the flurried.

Therefore the sage puts one foot in front of the other the entire day,

But never leaves his heavy pack behind.

Though there may be glorious sights at hand,

His course remains high and detached, as smooth as the flight of a swallow.

How will a lord of ten thousand chariots fool with his empire as though he himself had nothing to lose?

Act lightly and you lose your rootedness.

Act in a flurried way and you lose your command.

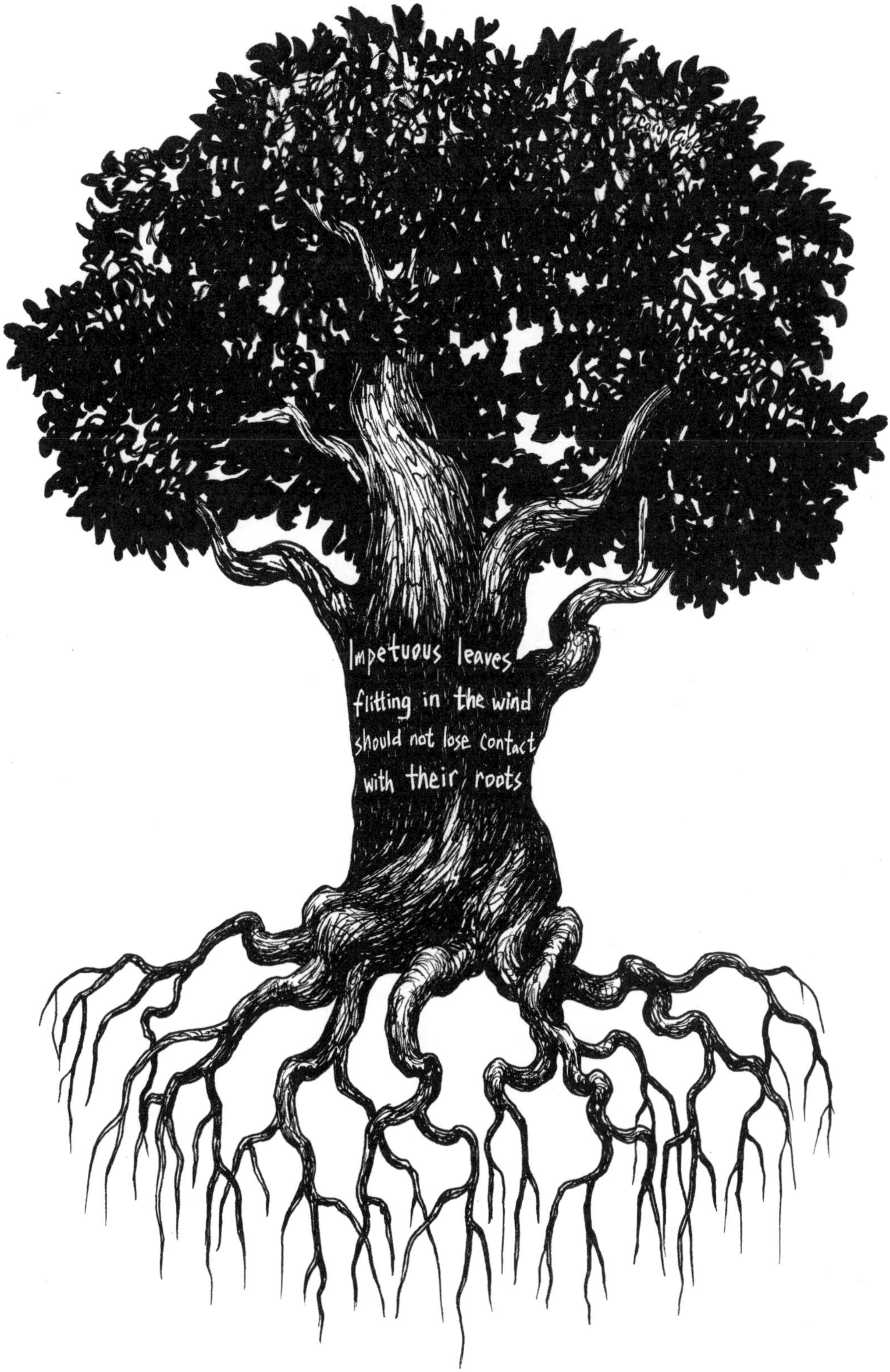

Impetuous leaves
flitting in the wind
should not lose contact
with their roots

# 27

Auspicious traveling leaves neither ruts nor tracks.

Auspicious words have neither flaws nor points for blame.

Auspicious calculation needs neither bamboo markers nor receipts.

The auspiciously shut has neither bolt nor key, but cannot be opened.

The auspiciously fastened uses neither rope nor binder, but cannot be untied.

Therefore the sage

> Always saves men from their mistakes in a goodly fashion,

> And thus no one is thrown overboard;

> Always saves things from their flaws in a skillful way,

> And thus none are tossed away.

This is called doubling and tripling your clarity.

In this way the adroit are the teachers of the clumsy,

And the clumsy are a wealth of raw material for the adroit.

If you do not treasure your teacher or show kindness to your raw material,

You will be shortsighted though you have the wisdom to predict the rain.

This is called the pivotal mystery.

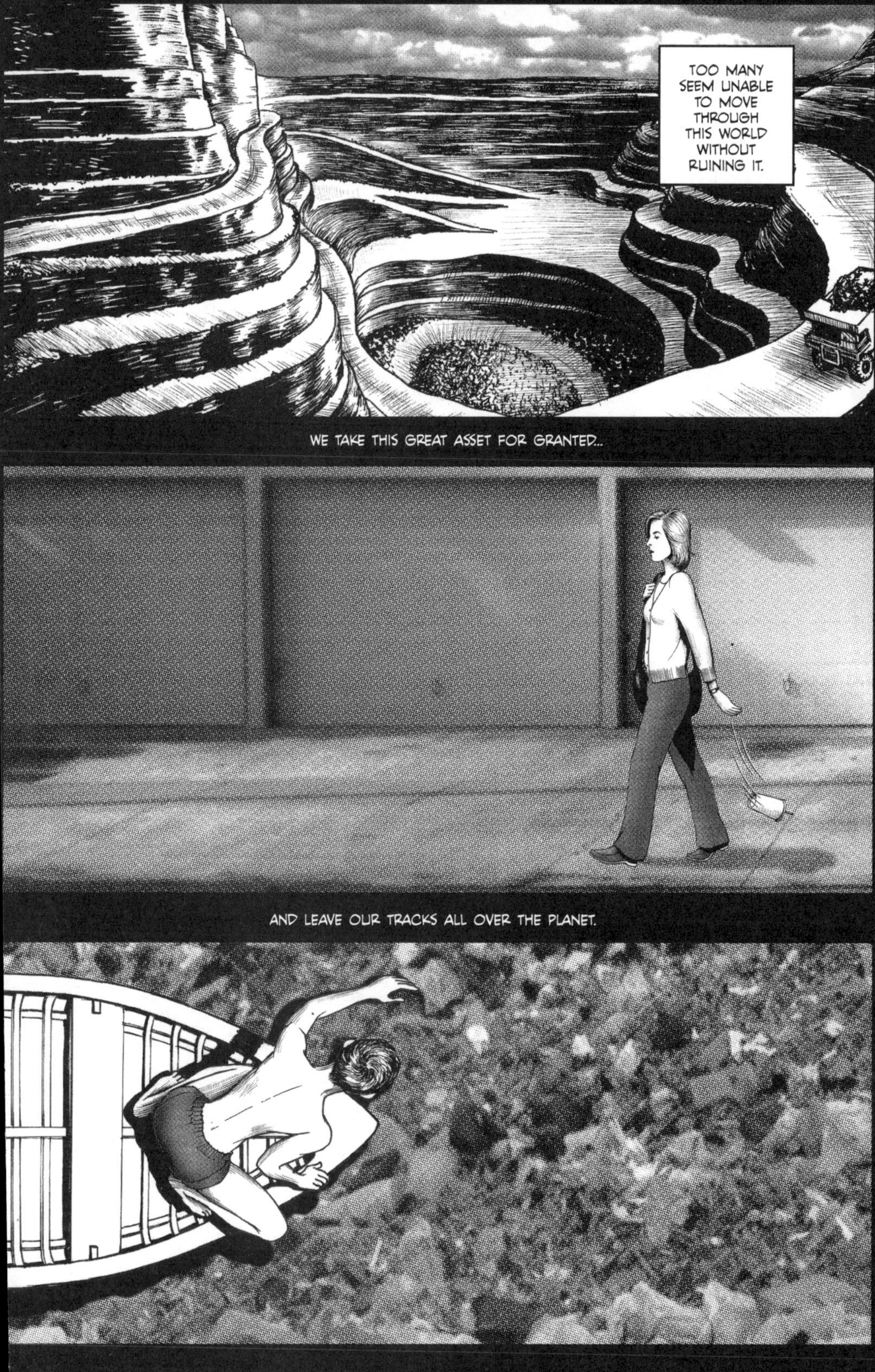
TOO MANY SEEM UNABLE TO MOVE THROUGH THIS WORLD WITHOUT RUINING IT.
WE TAKE THIS GREAT ASSET FOR GRANTED...
AND LEAVE OUR TRACKS ALL OVER THE PLANET.

# 28

If you know the male but preserve the female,

You will effect a mountain stream for all under heaven.

Effecting a mountain stream for all under heaven,

You will stay close to the Unchanging virtue

And be restored to the state of a suckling child.

If you know the bright but preserve the dark,

You will effect a model for all under heaven.

Effecting a model for all under heaven,

You will not run counter to the Unchanging virtue

And will be restored to That-Without-Limit.

If you know the flourishing but preserve the retiring,

You will effect a valley for all under heaven.

Effecting a valley for all under heaven,

Your Unchanging virtue will not be lacking

And you will be restored to a state of plain, unfinished wood.

When plain, unfinished wood is broken up into pieces,

The pieces may be fashioned into utensils.

If the "wise man" uses these, they will be fashioned into bureaucrats.

For this reason, the Great Preparer of things does not break them up.

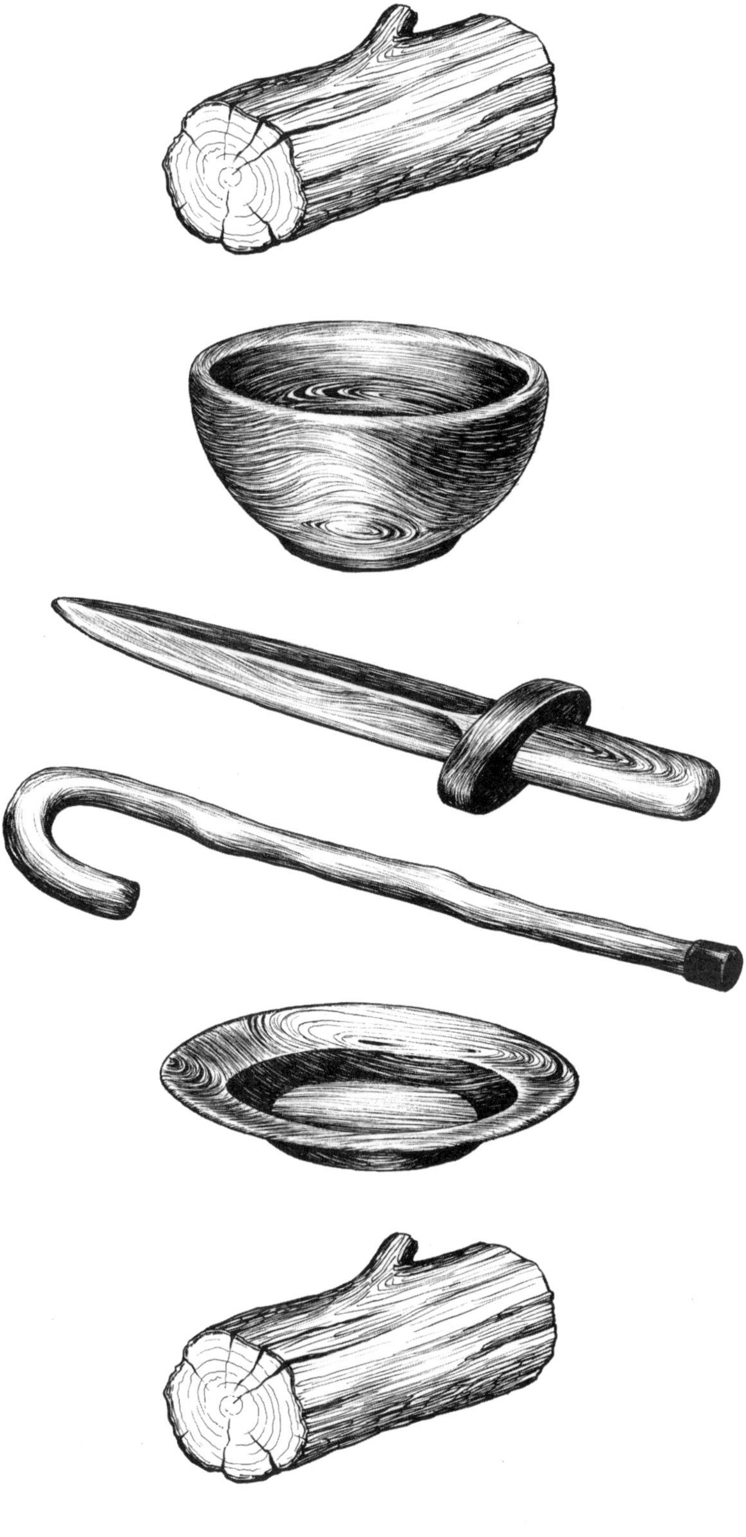

# 29

When a man wishes to take the world and make something of it,

I perceive that this will only end in failure.

The world is an instrument regulated by the gods,

And cannot be fabricated into something else.

He who tries to do this will damage it.

He who tries to grasp it will lose it.

Thus, as for the creatures of this world,

> There are those who step forward, and those who follow;

> There are those who breathe through their noses, and those who breathe through their mouths.

> There are those as strong as the sting of a wasp, and those as delicate as a sickly sheep.

> There are those who are thrown down, and those who fall down on their own.

Therefore the sage

> Avoids the extreme,

> Avoids the arrogant and self-willed,

> And avoids the excessive.

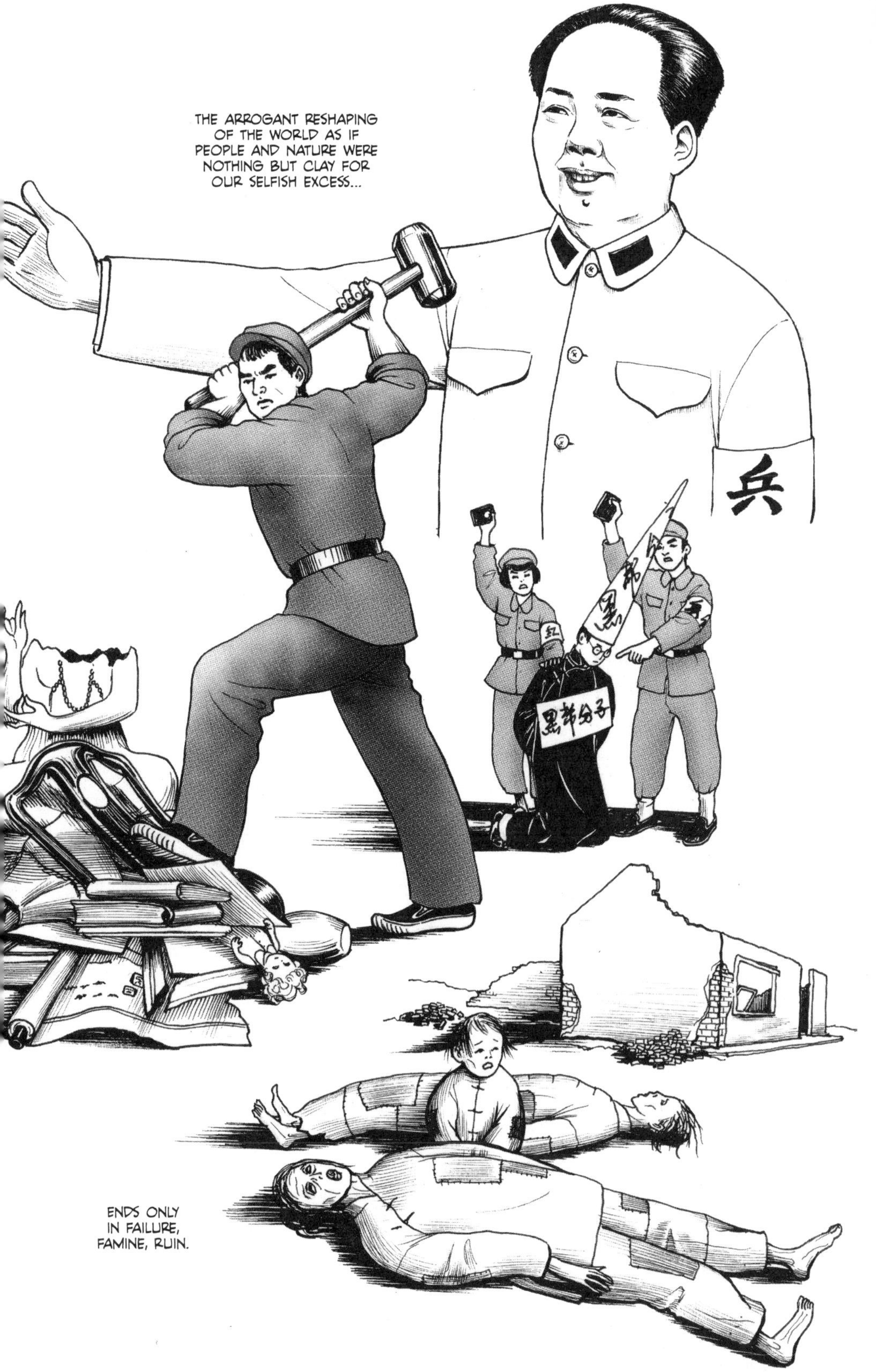
THE ARROGANT RESHAPING OF THE WORLD AS IF PEOPLE AND NATURE WERE NOTHING BUT CLAY FOR OUR SELFISH EXCESS...
兵
黑帮分子
ENDS ONLY IN FAILURE, FAMINE, RUIN.

# 30

He who would wholeheartedly help the ruler of men by means of the Way

Will not use military weapons to force himself on the world.

In putting his hands to things, he prefers returning to the fundamental Way.

Wherever troops bivouac, thorny shrubs and spiny brambles grow.

After the clashes of great armies, years of empty fields and hungry mouths will inevitably be at hand.

The man adroit at government only brings affairs to fruition as fruit will grow on trees.

He does not dare to grasp in order to strengthen.

Bringing affairs to fruition, he does not make much of himself.

Bringing affairs to fruition, he does not contend.

Bringing affairs to fruition, he does not look down on others.

Bringing affairs to fruition, he does so only when it can't be helped.

Bringing affairs to fruition, he does not force others.

After creatures reach their peak, they begin to grow bent and old.

This is said not to be following the Way.

Those who do not follow the Way soon come to an end.

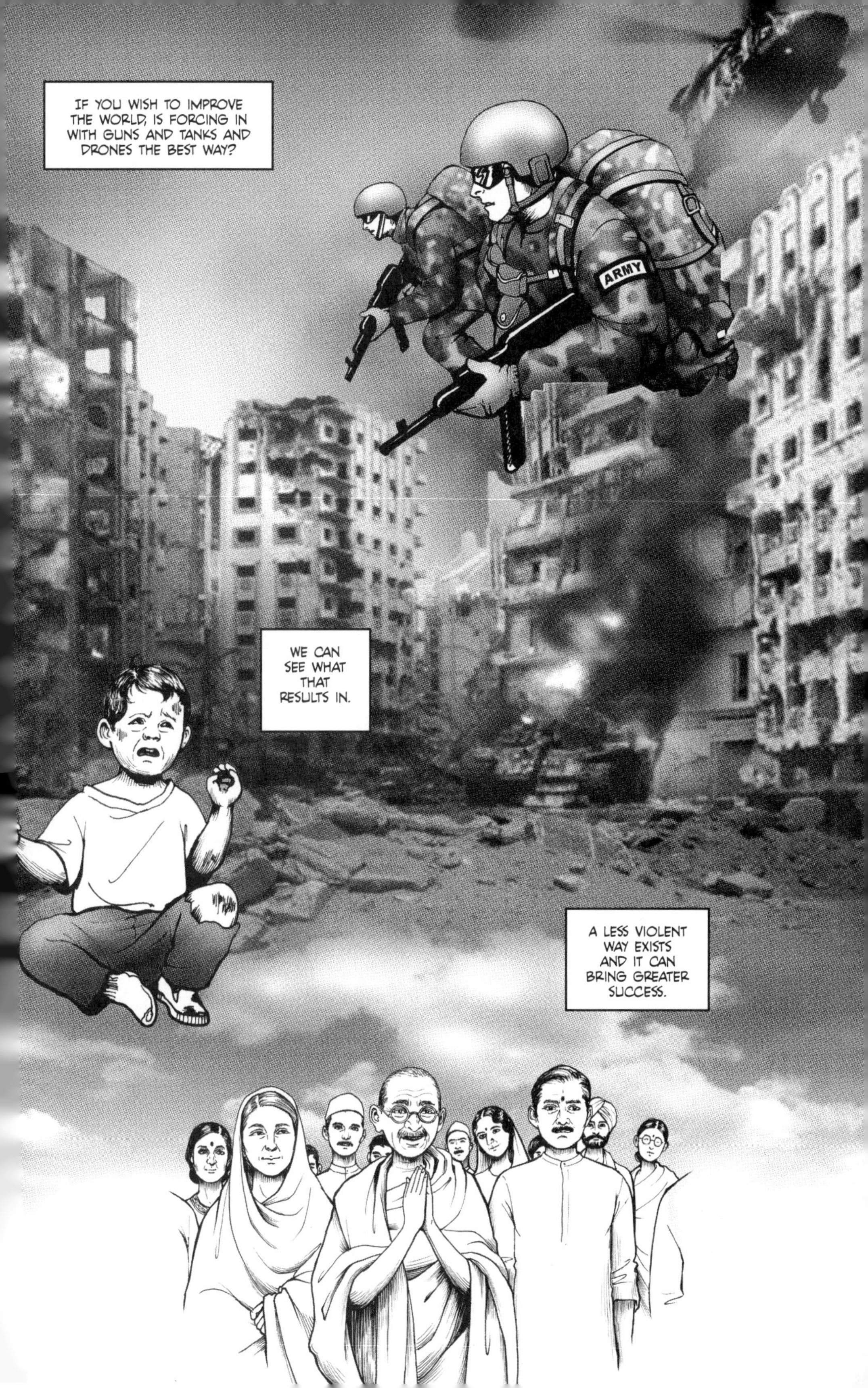
IF YOU WISH TO IMPROVE THE WORLD, IS FORCING IN WITH GUNS AND TANKS AND DRONES THE BEST WAY?
ARMY
WE CAN SEE WHAT THAT RESULTS IN.
A LESS VIOLENT WAY EXISTS AND IT CAN BRING GREATER SUCCESS.

# 31

Listen, well-polished weapons are inauspicious tools;

All creatures consistently back away from them.

Thus, a man who possesses the Way will not have
them around.

When the Gentleman is at home, he keeps them at his left;

But when in use, he keeps them at his right.


But weapons are inauspicious tools,

And they are not the tools of the Gentleman.

He uses them only when it can't be helped,

And considers tranquility and simplicity to be the
highest good.

Victory he does not find beautiful,

For to do so would be to enjoy killing others.

And listen, the man who enjoys killing others

Will find his ambitions thwarted in this world.


In auspicious matters, you honor the left;

In inauspicious matters, you honor the right.

A company commander will occupy the left;

The commander-in-chief will occupy the right.

Which is to say that their formation is proper to that
of a funeral.


When many people are killed

We shed tears in pity and grief.

For victory in battle, we take a stance proper to
funeral rites.

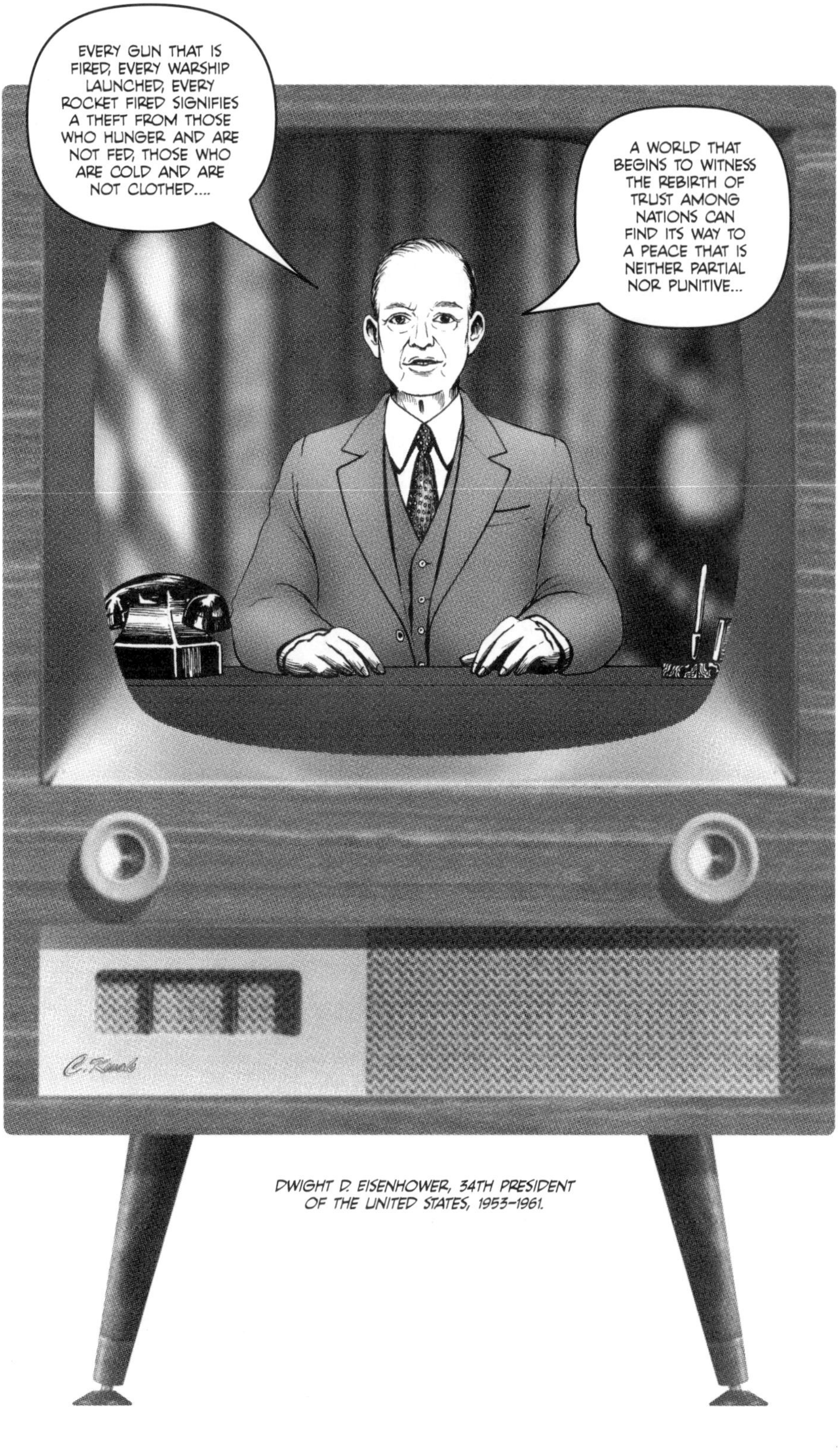
EVERY GUN THAT IS FIRED, EVERY WARSHIP LAUNCHED, EVERY ROCKET FIRED SIGNIFIES A THEFT FROM THOSE WHO HUNGER AND ARE NOT FED, THOSE WHO ARE COLD AND ARE NOT CLOTHED....
A WORLD THAT BEGINS TO WITNESS THE REBIRTH OF TRUST AMONG NATIONS CAN FIND ITS WAY TO A PEACE THAT IS NEITHER PARTIAL NOR PUNITIVE...

*DWIGHT D. EISENHOWER, 34TH PRESIDENT OF THE UNITED STATES, 1953–1961.*

# 32

The Way is unchanging and is without name.

Though its unvarnished state may seem of little account,

It is subordinate to nothing in this world.

If lords and kings were able to keep it in store,

The Ten Thousand Things would surely follow their lead.

Heaven and Earth mutually unite, and sweet dew descends.

Without people's command, it falls equally of its own accord.

When you begin to divide and arrange, names are at hand;

And when names are already at hand,

You should know that it's time to stop.

It is by knowing when to stop that you will not tread on dangerous ground.

To give a comparison, the Way's existence in the world

Is like rivers and streams flowing into inlets and seas.

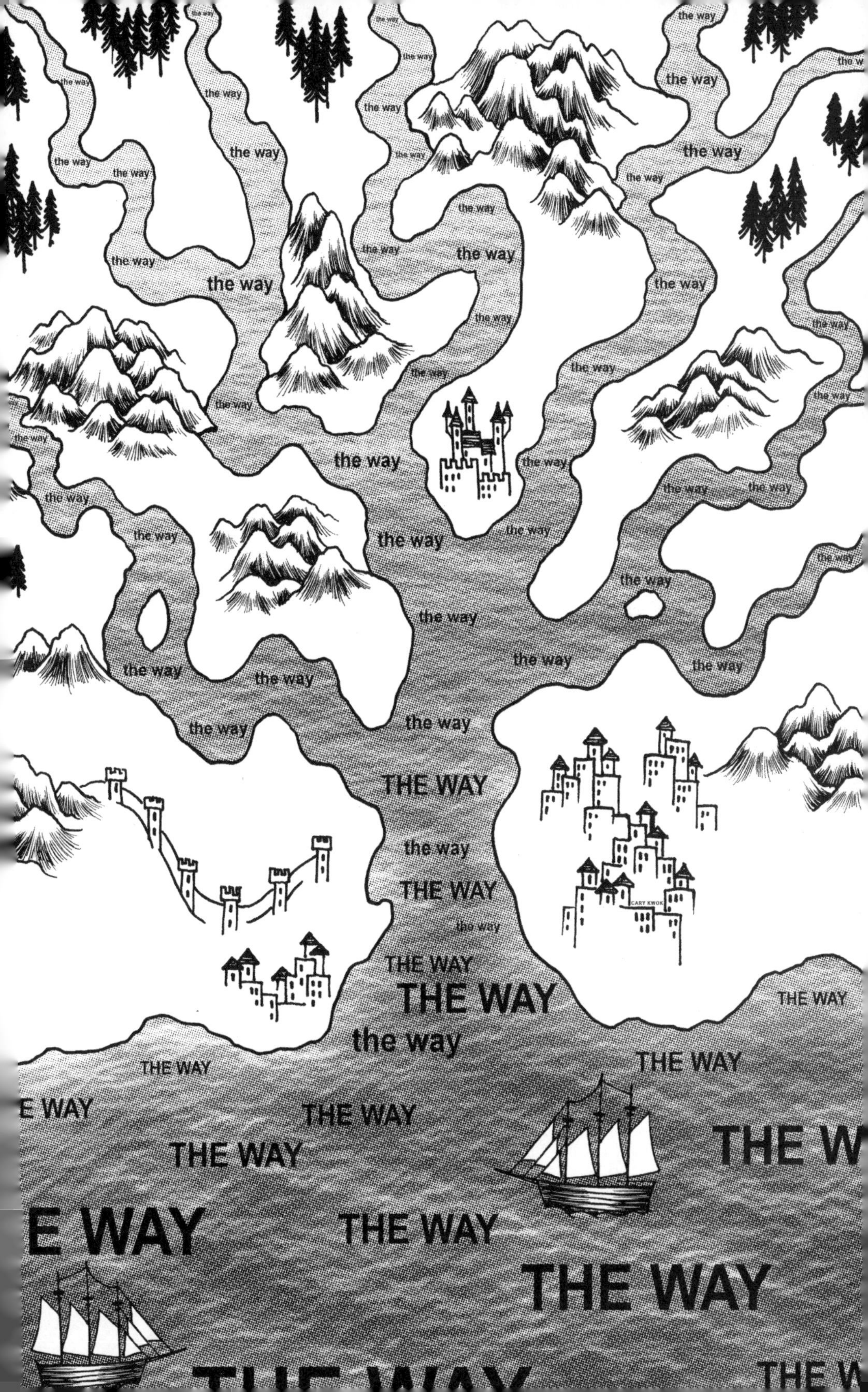

the way
the way
the way
the way
the way
the way
the way
the way
the way
the way
the way
the way
the way
the way
the way
the way
the way
the way
the way
the way
the way
the way
the way
the way
the way
the way
the way
the way
the way
the way
the way
the way
the way
the way
the way
the way
the way
the way
the way
THE WAY
the way
THE WAY
CARY KWOK
the way
THE WAY
THE WAY
THE WAY
the way
THE WAY
THE WAY
E WAY
THE WAY
THE WAY
THE W
E WAY
THE WAY
THE WAY
THE W

# 33

He who knows others may have knowledge enough to predict the rain,

But he who knows himself will see with the clarity of the sun and moon.

He who is victorious over others has strength,

But he who is victorious over himself will have the potency of a swarm of bees.

He who knows how to stop with what is sufficient is rich with his own house and fields,

And he who puts one foot in front of the other with strength will have resolution.

He who does not lose his place will stay long,

And he who dies but is not forgotten will be long-lived.

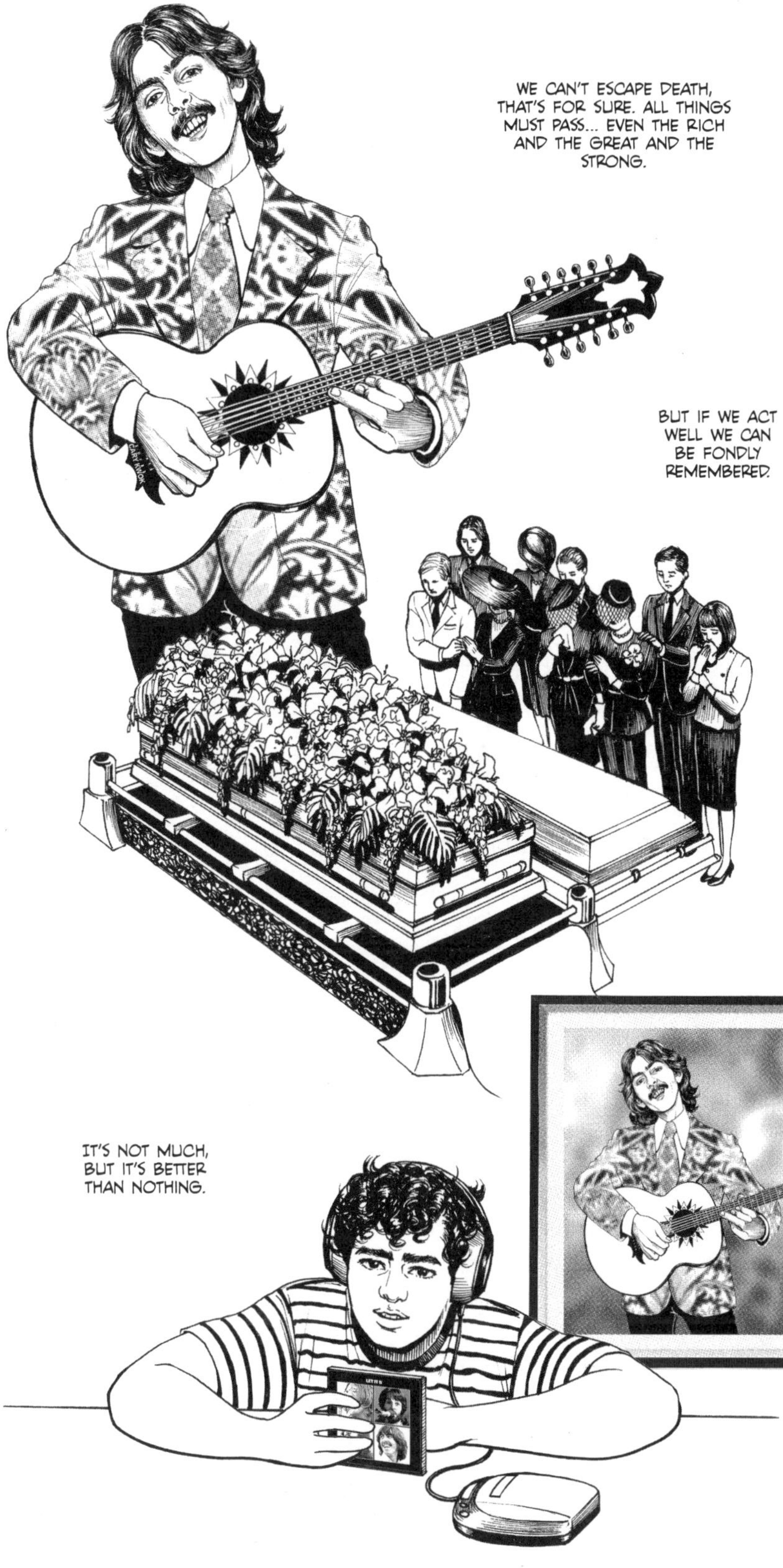
WE CAN'T ESCAPE DEATH, THAT'S FOR SURE. ALL THINGS MUST PASS... EVEN THE RICH AND THE GREAT AND THE STRONG.
BUT IF WE ACT WELL WE CAN BE FONDLY REMEMBERED.
IT'S NOT MUCH, BUT IT'S BETTER THAN NOTHING.

# 34

The Way drifts buoyantly, now left, now right.

The Ten Thousand Things rely on it, and are born without fanfare.

It does good work, but does not hold on to fame.

It clothes and nourishes the Ten Thousand Things, but does not assume to be their master.

As it is always without desire, you might name it the Insignificant.

The Ten Thousand Things return to it, but do not consider it their master.

You could give it a name, and fashion it the Great,

But it does not consider itself great.

Thus it is able to achieve its magnitude.

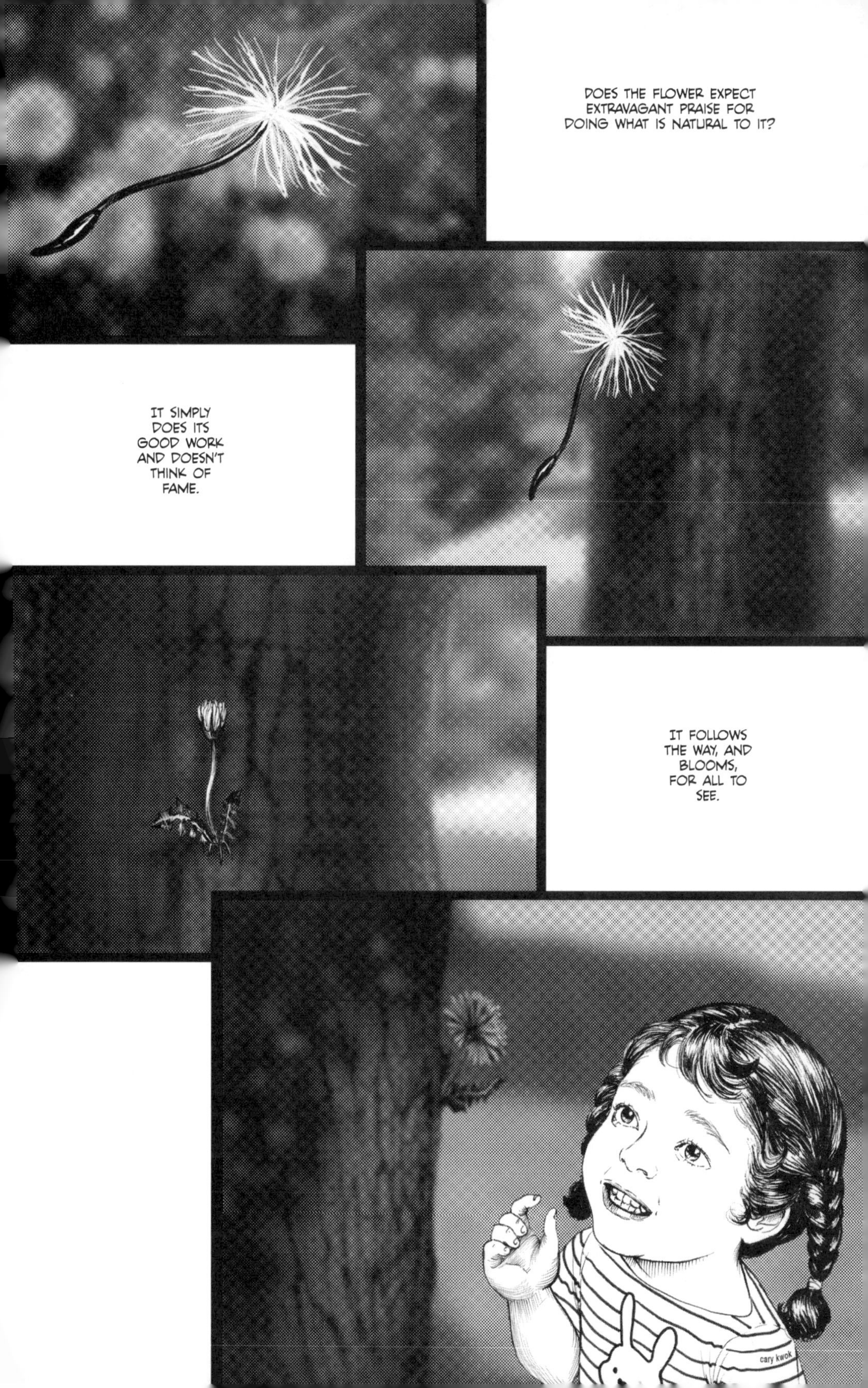
DOES THE FLOWER EXPECT EXTRAVAGANT PRAISE FOR DOING WHAT IS NATURAL TO IT?
IT SIMPLY DOES ITS GOOD WORK AND DOESN'T THINK OF FAME.
IT FOLLOWS THE WAY, AND BLOOMS, FOR ALL TO SEE.
cary kwok

# 35

If you shackle yourself to the Great Form,

And walk about in the world,

You may walk about without harm,

And with security, peace, and ease.

If there are stringed instruments and dumplings,

The traveler passing through will stop;

But what comes from the mouth of the Way

Is like thin soup without taste.

You may gaze at it fixedly, but there's little to see;

You may listen to it intently, but there's little to hear;

You may use it all you like, and it will never be used up.

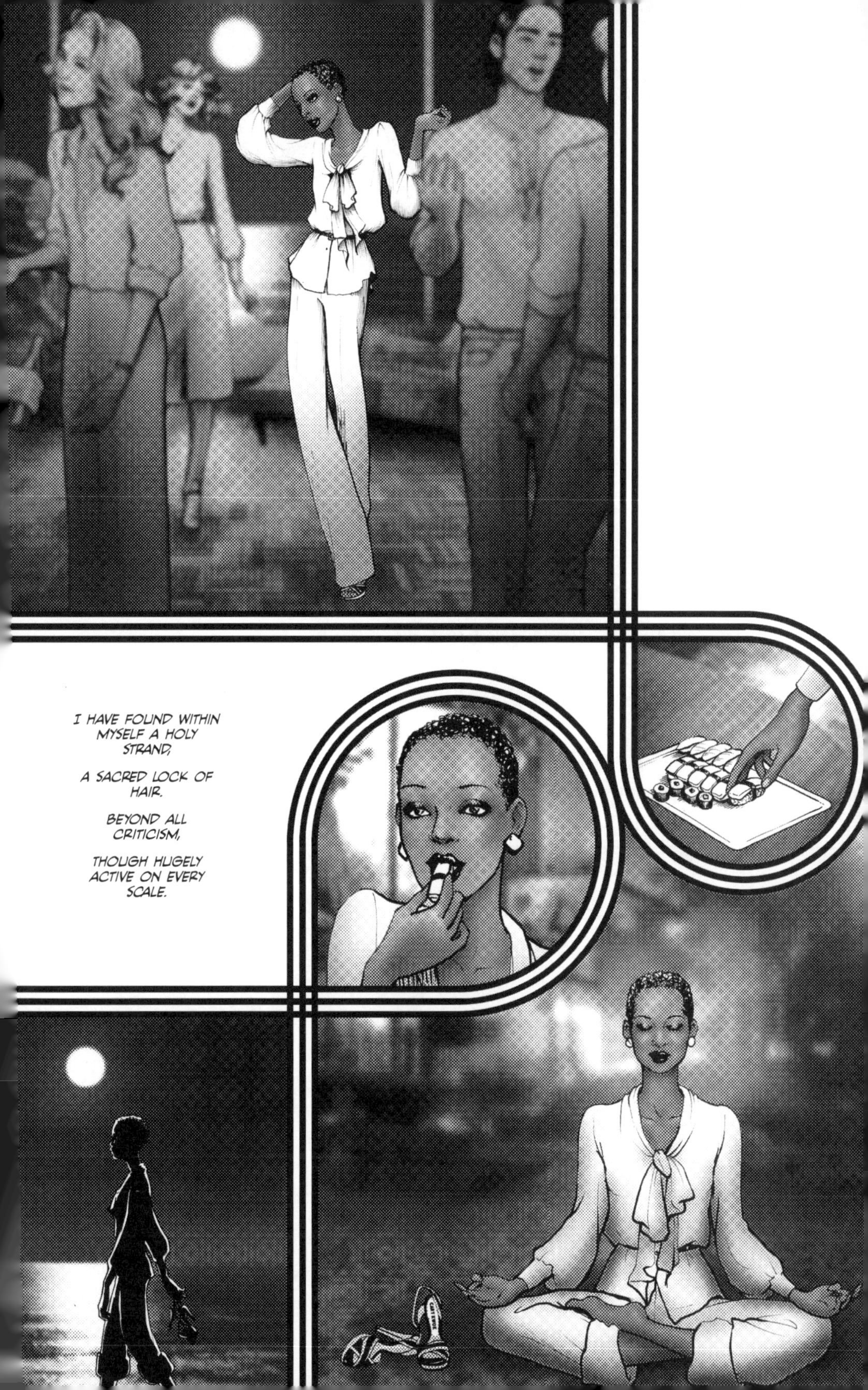
I HAVE FOUND WITHIN MYSELF A HOLY STRAND,
A SACRED LOCK OF HAIR.
BEYOND ALL CRITICISM,
THOUGH HUGELY ACTIVE ON EVERY SCALE.

# 36

If you wish to draw in your wings,

You must momentarily stretch them out.

If you wish to weaken something,

You must momentarily make it strong.

If you wish to bring something lower,

You must momentarily lift it up.

If you wish to grasp something,

You must momentarily give it up.

This is called "the something hidden in the brightness of day."

The soft and weak will be victorious over the hard and strong.


Fish should not be taken from their deep pools;

The country's sharp weapons and clever administrators should not be shown to the people.

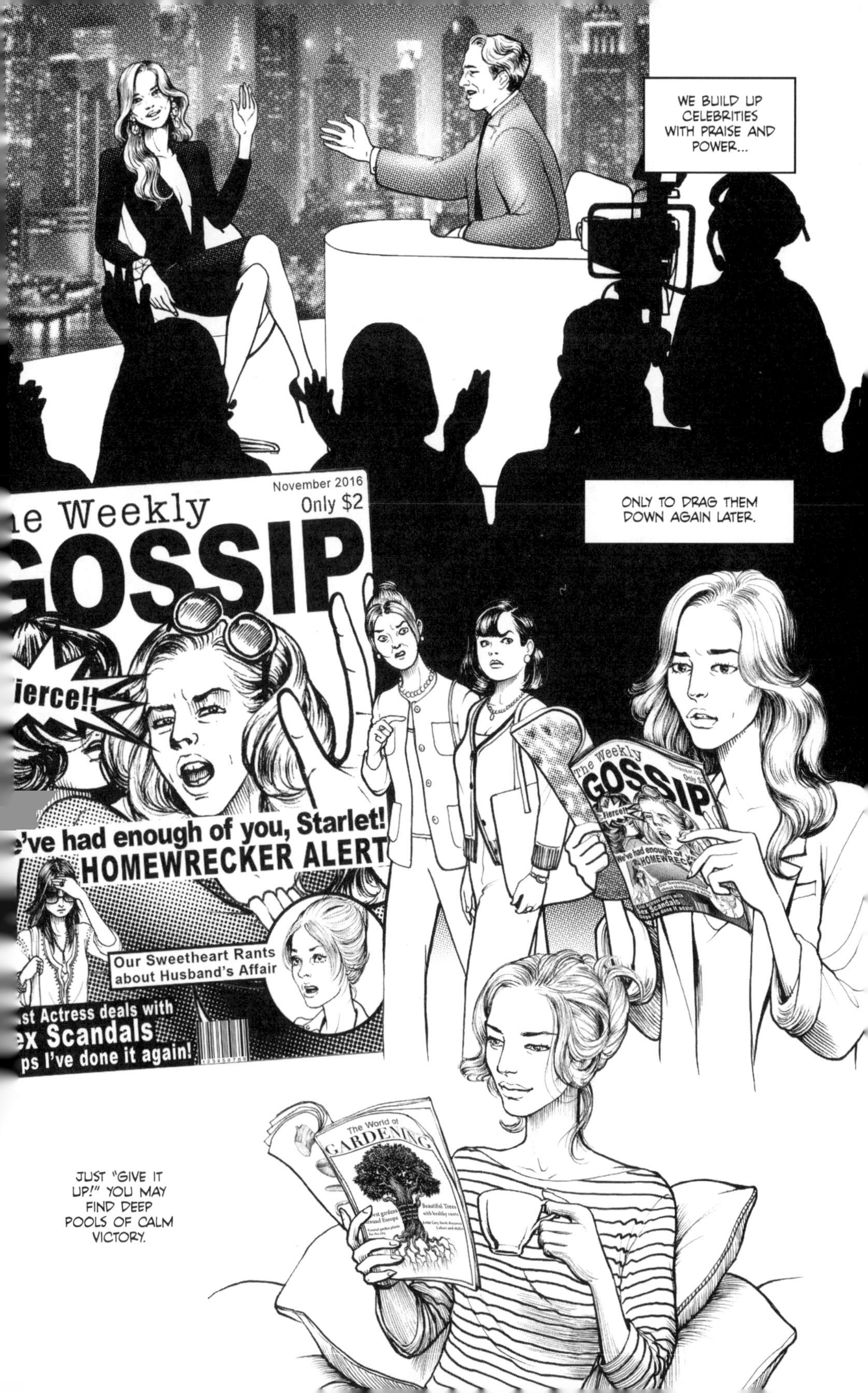
WE BUILD UP CELEBRITIES WITH PRAISE AND POWER...
ONLY TO DRAG THEM DOWN AGAIN LATER.
November 2016
Only $2
e Weekly
GOSSIP
ierce!!
e've had enough of you, Starlet!
HOMEWRECKER ALERT
Our Sweetheart Rants about Husband's Affair
st Actress deals with
ex Scandals
ps I've done it again!
The Weekly
GOSSIP
The World of
GARDENING
Beautiful Trees
with healthy roots
JUST "GIVE IT UP!" YOU MAY FIND DEEP POOLS OF CALM VICTORY.

# 37

The Way never acts,

Yet no act is left undone.

If lords and kings were able to maintain this,

The Ten Thousand Things would transform on their own.

If, once transforming, desire were to arise,

I would calm this desire with an unvarnished simplicity
that has no name.

Listen, with this unvarnished simplicity without a name

There will be no desires.

Without desires, there will be peace,

And all under heaven will be settled on its own.

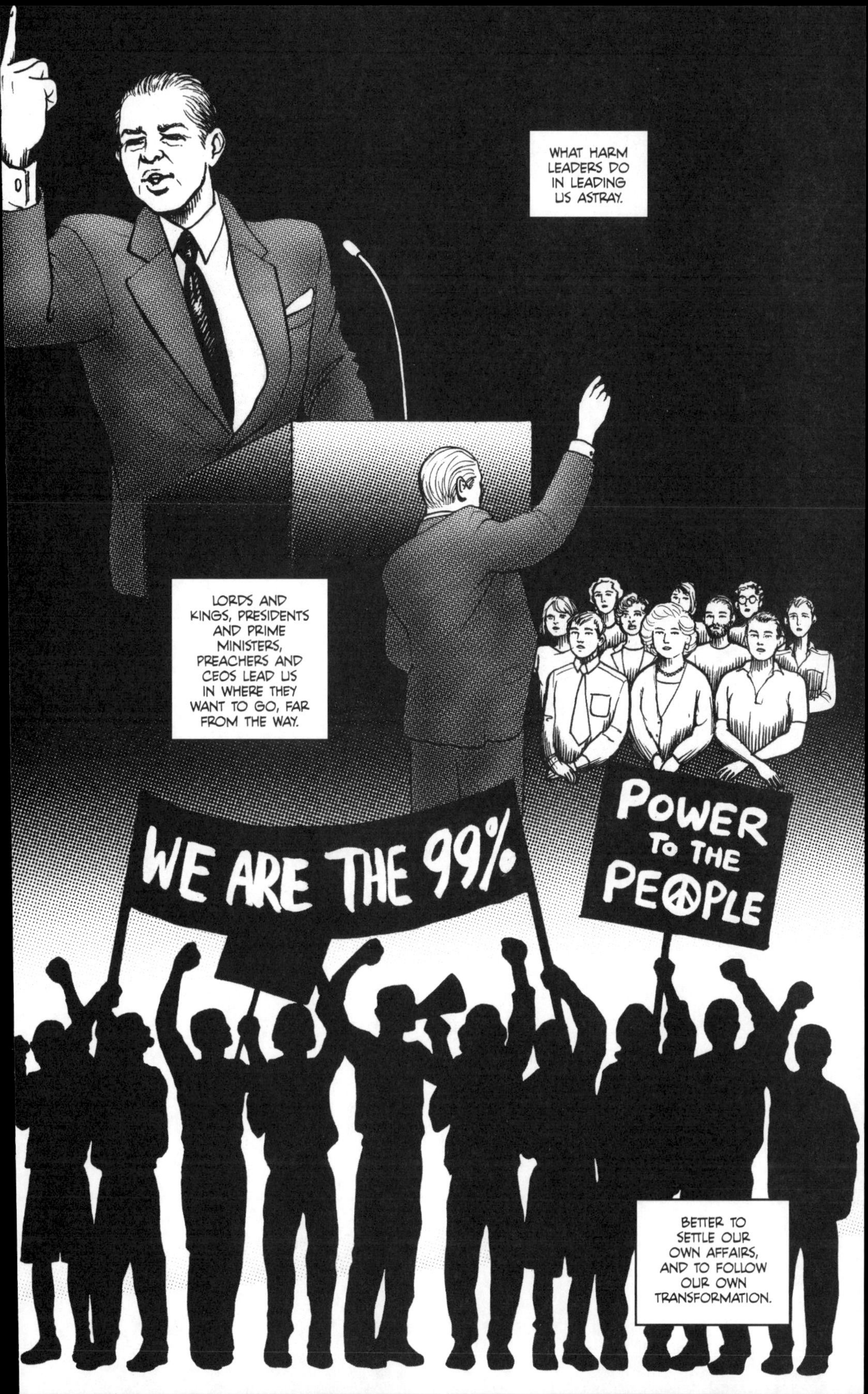
WHAT HARM LEADERS DO IN LEADING US ASTRAY.
LORDS AND KINGS, PRESIDENTS AND PRIME MINISTERS, PREACHERS AND CEOS LEAD US IN WHERE THEY WANT TO GO, FAR FROM THE WAY.
WE ARE THE 99%
POWER TO THE PEOPLE
BETTER TO SETTLE OUR OWN AFFAIRS, AND TO FOLLOW OUR OWN TRANSFORMATION.

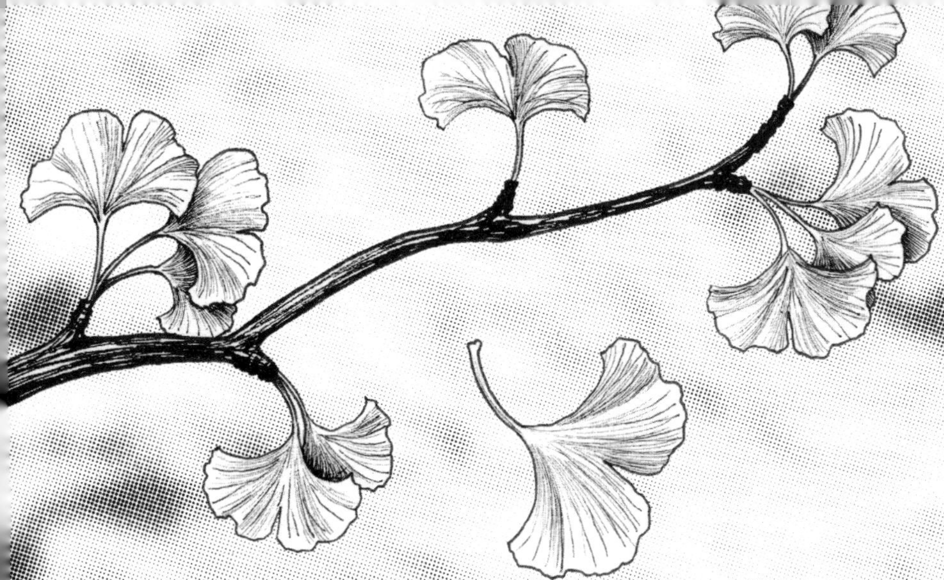

# CANTO 2

# THE BOOK OF VIRTUE

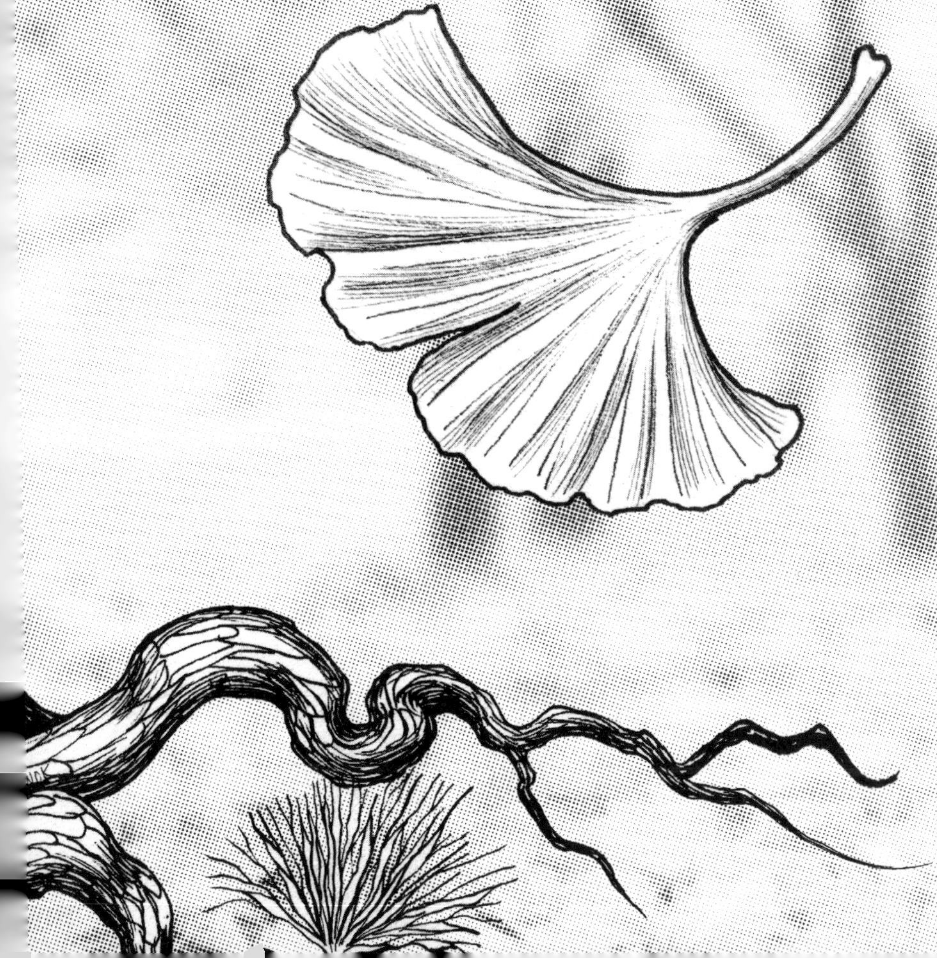

# 38

The highest virtue does not act virtuously;

Therefore, virtue is at hand.

The lowest virtue won't let go of virtue;

Therefore, it has none.

The highest virtue does not act according to form,

So nothing is fabricated.

The lowest virtue acts according to form,

So everything is fabricated.

The highest human-heartedness acts according to form,

Yet nothing is fabricated.

The highest righteousness acts according to form,

So everything is fabricated.

The highest etiquette acts according to form,

And if there is no proper response,

Rolls up its sleeves and presses on.

Thus, lose the Way, and virtue will come up from behind;

Lose virtue, and human-heartedness will come up
from behind;

Lose human-heartedness, and righteousness will come
up from behind.

Lose righteousness, and you'll get good manners.

Listen, a person with good manners

Is thin on loyalty and standing by his word,

And this is the headwaters of disorder.

Consciousness before action

Creates the flower of the Way

And is the beginning of circuitous thinking.

Therefore, the man of character

Will sit down with the grounded,

But will not associate with the light-headed;

Will sit down with the fruit,

But will not associate with the flower.

Thus, he avoids the one, and takes the other.

# 39

Of those who obtained the One along the way in ancient times:

Heaven obtained the One, and became transparent;

Earth obtained the One, and became pacified;

The spirits obtained the One, and were imbued with the essential mystery of things;

The valleys obtained the One, and were filled to the brim;

The Ten Thousand Things obtained the One, and sprouted with life;

Lords and kings obtained the One, and divined how to make the world correct.

It was the One that guided them along.

If Heaven were not transparent,

I'm afraid it would soon be rent like cloth.

If Earth were not pacified,

I'm afraid it would soon begin to shake.

If the spirits were not imbued with the essential
mystery of things,

I'm afraid they would soon not bother to exert
themselves.

If the valleys were not filled to the brim,

I'm afraid they would soon be dried up.

If the Ten Thousand Things did not sprout with life,

I'm afraid they would soon become parched and wither.

If lords and kings were not respected and on high,

I'm afraid they would soon stumble and fall.


Thus, that which is of little value creates the
foundation for that which is treasured,

And that which is low creates a bedrock for that which
is high.

Therefore, lords and kings call themselves orphans,
widowers, and menials.

Is this not making what is of little value the foundation?

Is this not so?

Thus, though you may often be awarded words of
praise, you will have no honor.

Do not wish to jangle like jewels;

Rather, resonate like rocks and stones.

# 40

Return is the movement of the Way;

The weak and flexible is the function of the Way.

The Ten Thousand Things of the world are born from existence;

Existence is born from nonexistence.

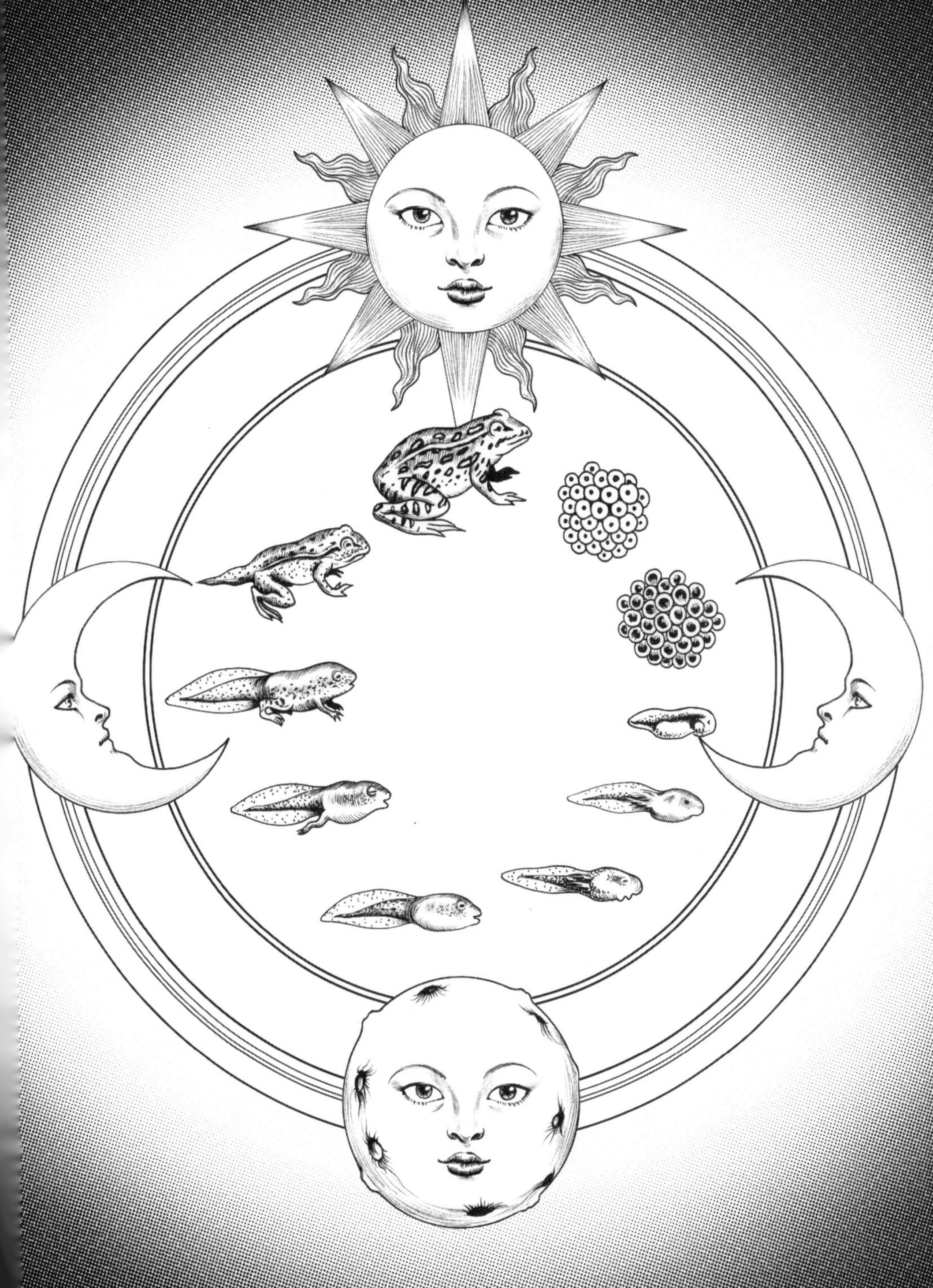

# 41

When the best kind of educated Gentleman hears of the Way,

He braces himself, puts effort into it, and behaves accordingly.

When the middling kind hears of the Way,

He thinks maybe it exists, but maybe it doesn't.

When the lowest type hears of the Way,

He gives a belly laugh.

If he did not laugh,

It would not suffice to be considered the Way.

Thus, there are these lodestar sayings:

The Way, as bright as the sun and moon, is like the darkness before dawn.

When the Way advances, it seems to be retreating.

The Way that subdues and makes all things even seems to be tangled and ambiguous.

The highest virtue seems like the empty mouth of a valley.

That which is immaculate seems muddy and unclear.

An open and unblocked virtue seems unapproachable.

Established virtue seems provisional.

The rock-solid truth seems as changeable as flowing water.

The great square of the Earth has no corners.

A great vessel is made over time.

A great sound has a rare voice.

A great form is without shape.

The Way is hidden and without an identifying name.

Listen, it is only the Way that attends to the intrinsic value of things well, and then brings them to completion.

# 42

The Way gives birth to the One;

The One gives birth to the Two;

The Two gives birth to the Three;

The Three gives birth to the Ten Thousand Things.

The Ten Thousand Things carry the Yin and enfold the Yang;

Kneading them gently, they create harmony.

What people dislike is to be orphaned, widowed, or to become menials.

Still, kings and princes account themselves as such.

Thus at times, creatures suffer decrease, and yet increase.

At times they increase, and yet suffer decrease.

What people exhort,

I do as well:

The strong and self-assertive will not achieve the death they would like.

This teaching I would make the keeper of the sacred fire.

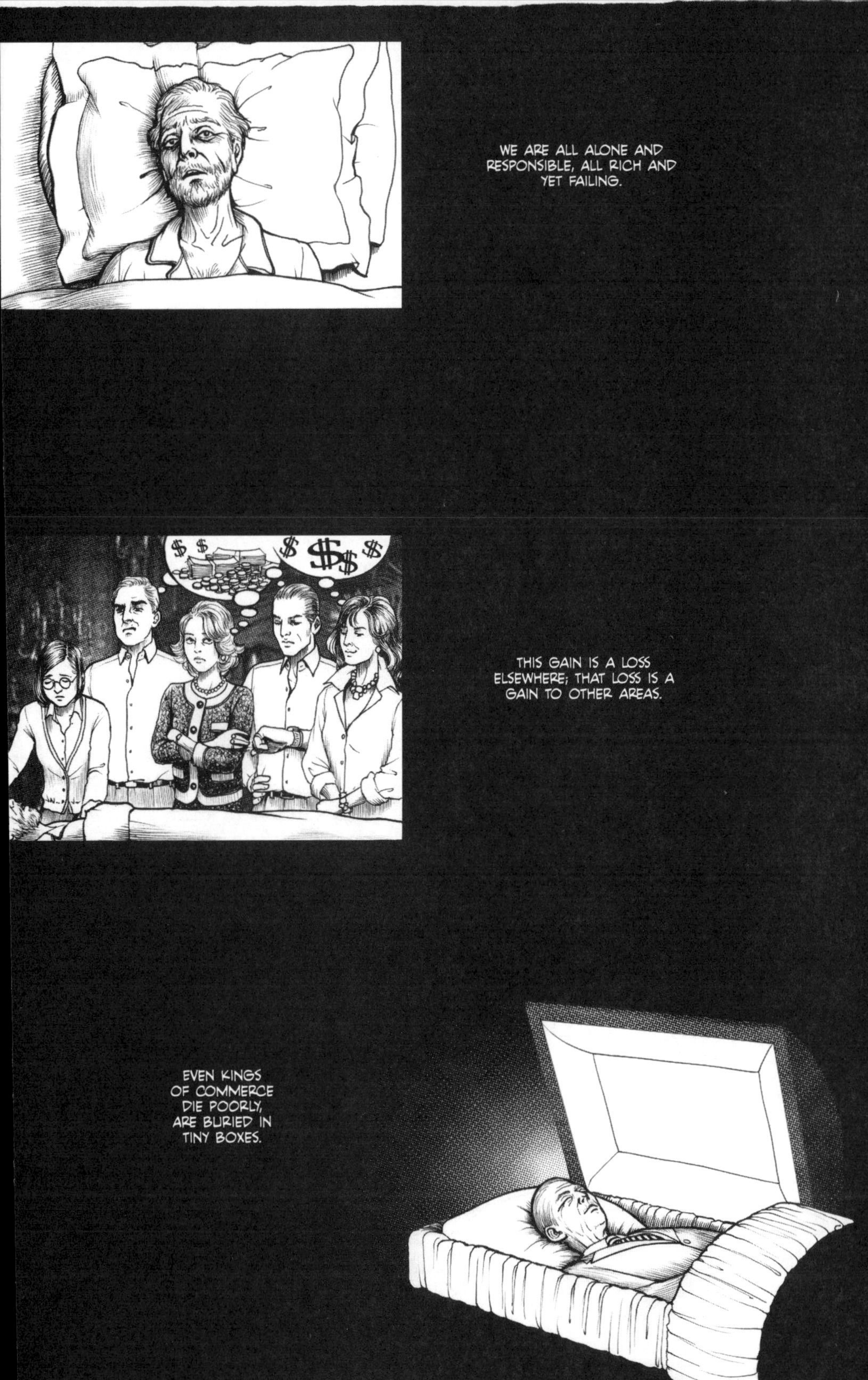
WE ARE ALL ALONE AND RESPONSIBLE, ALL RICH AND YET FAILING.
THIS GAIN IS A LOSS ELSEWHERE; THAT LOSS IS A GAIN TO OTHER AREAS.
EVEN KINGS OF COMMERCE DIE POORLY, ARE BURIED IN TINY BOXES.

# 43

The softest in the world dominate the hardest just
as you would whip forward a horse.

That without form or substance enters where there is
no space at all.

By this I know beyond a doubt the fulfillment of
nonfabrication.

Wordless teaching, the fulfillment of nonfabrication:

In this world there are few who can grasp these.

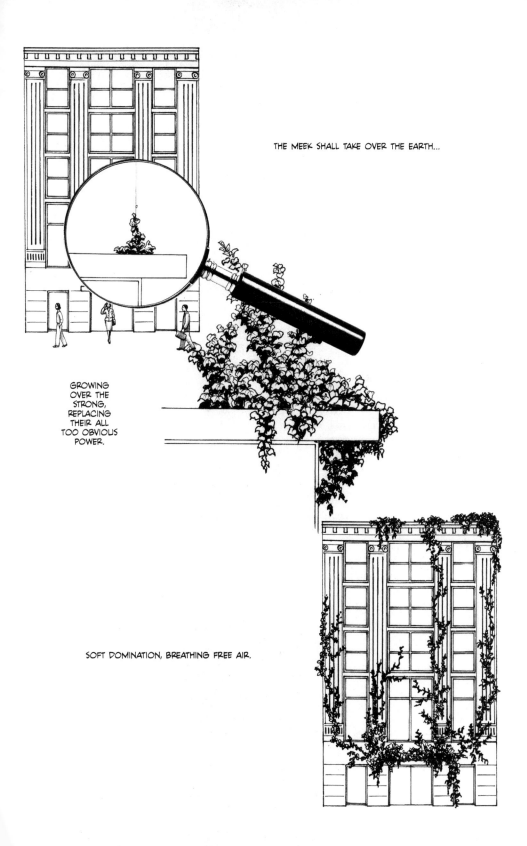

THE MEEK SHALL TAKE OVER THE EARTH...

GROWING
OVER THE
STRONG,
REPLACING
THEIR ALL
TOO OBVIOUS
POWER.

SOFT DOMINATION, BREATHING FREE AIR.

# 44

Your reputation or your physical self:

which do you see as your very life?

Your physical self or your capital:

which is better?

To pick up something along the way or to lose something:

which is more inductive to pain?

For these reasons, if you desire something excessively,

you will invariably have great expenses;

If you store many things away,

you will invariably lose things by the pile.

If you clearly know what is sufficient,

you will not be embarrassed;

If you know when to stop,

you will not stand on shaky ground.

Thus, you will be able to continue for a long time.

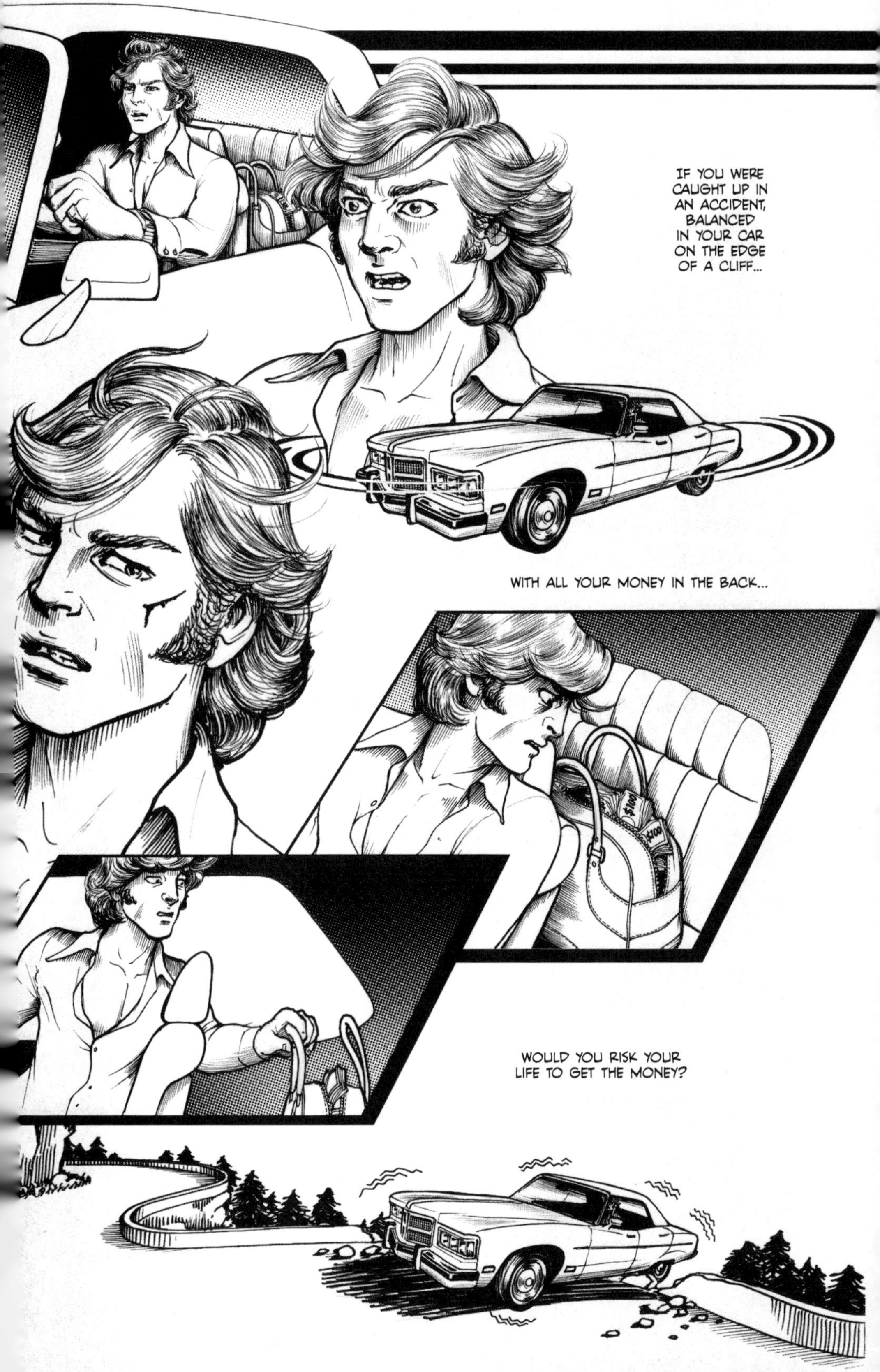
IF YOU WERE CAUGHT UP IN AN ACCIDENT, BALANCED IN YOUR CAR ON THE EDGE OF A CLIFF...
WITH ALL YOUR MONEY IN THE BACK...
$100
$100
WOULD YOU RISK YOUR LIFE TO GET THE MONEY?

# 45

Great accomplishment seems lacking,

But its use never fails.

A bowl filled to the top seems empty,

But its use never comes to an end.

The perfectly straight seems crooked;

Great skill seems like bungling;

Mellifluous speech seems tongue-tied.

Flurried movement defeats the cold;

Tranquility defeats the heat.

Clarity and tranquility make the world impartial.

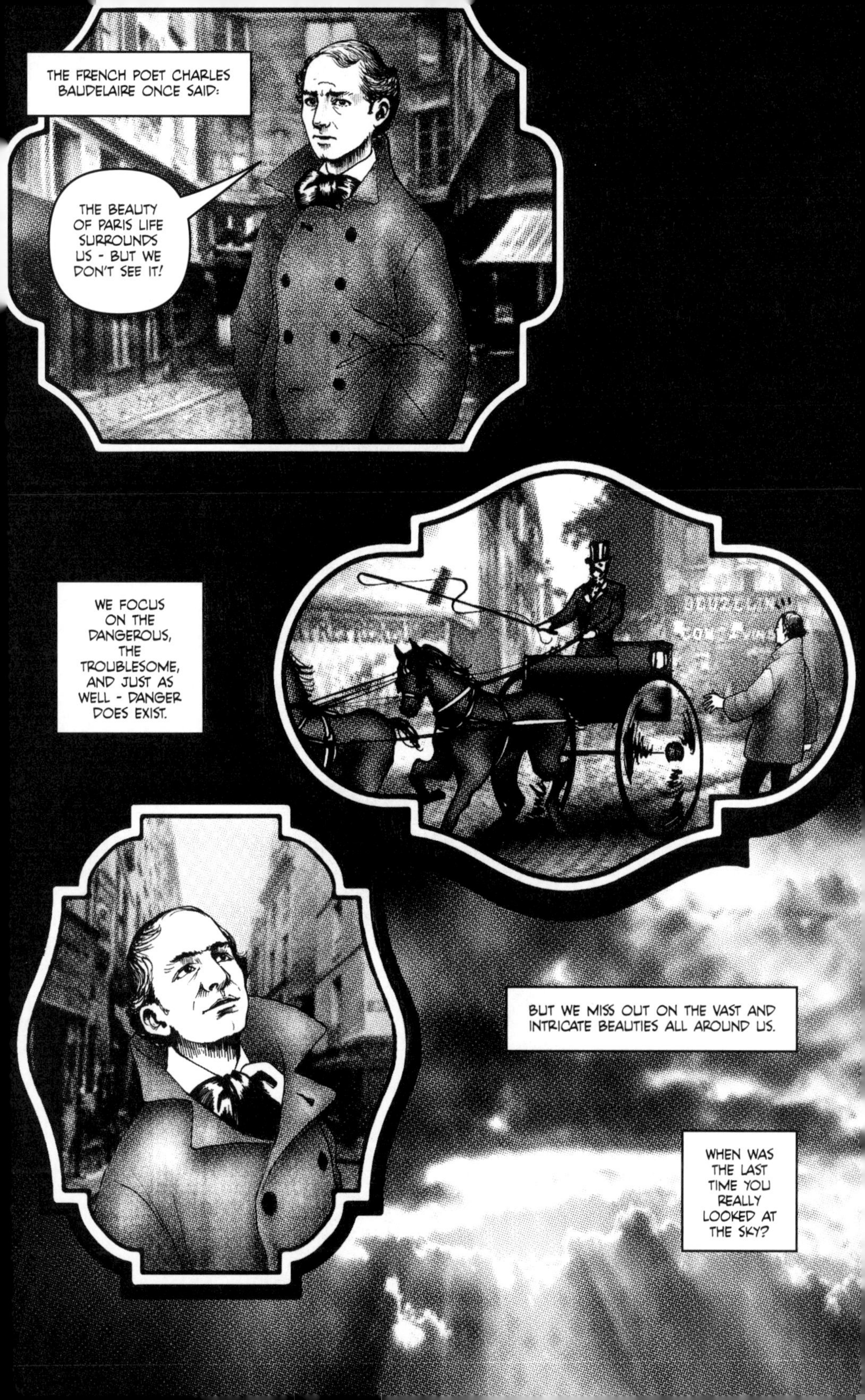
THE FRENCH POET CHARLES BAUDELAIRE ONCE SAID:
THE BEAUTY OF PARIS LIFE SURROUNDS US - BUT WE DON'T SEE IT!
WE FOCUS ON THE DANGEROUS, THE TROUBLESOME, AND JUST AS WELL - DANGER DOES EXIST.
BUT WE MISS OUT ON THE VAST AND INTRICATE BEAUTIES ALL AROUND US.
WHEN WAS THE LAST TIME YOU REALLY LOOKED AT THE SKY?

# 46

When the Way is at hand in the world,

Running horses are led back to the fields to create manure.

When the Way is not in the world,

Generations of horses are born within the borders of the state.

There is no disaster greater than not knowing what is enough.

There is no fault greater than wanting to obtain more.

Thus, the sufficiency of knowing what is sufficient

Is unchangingly sufficient!

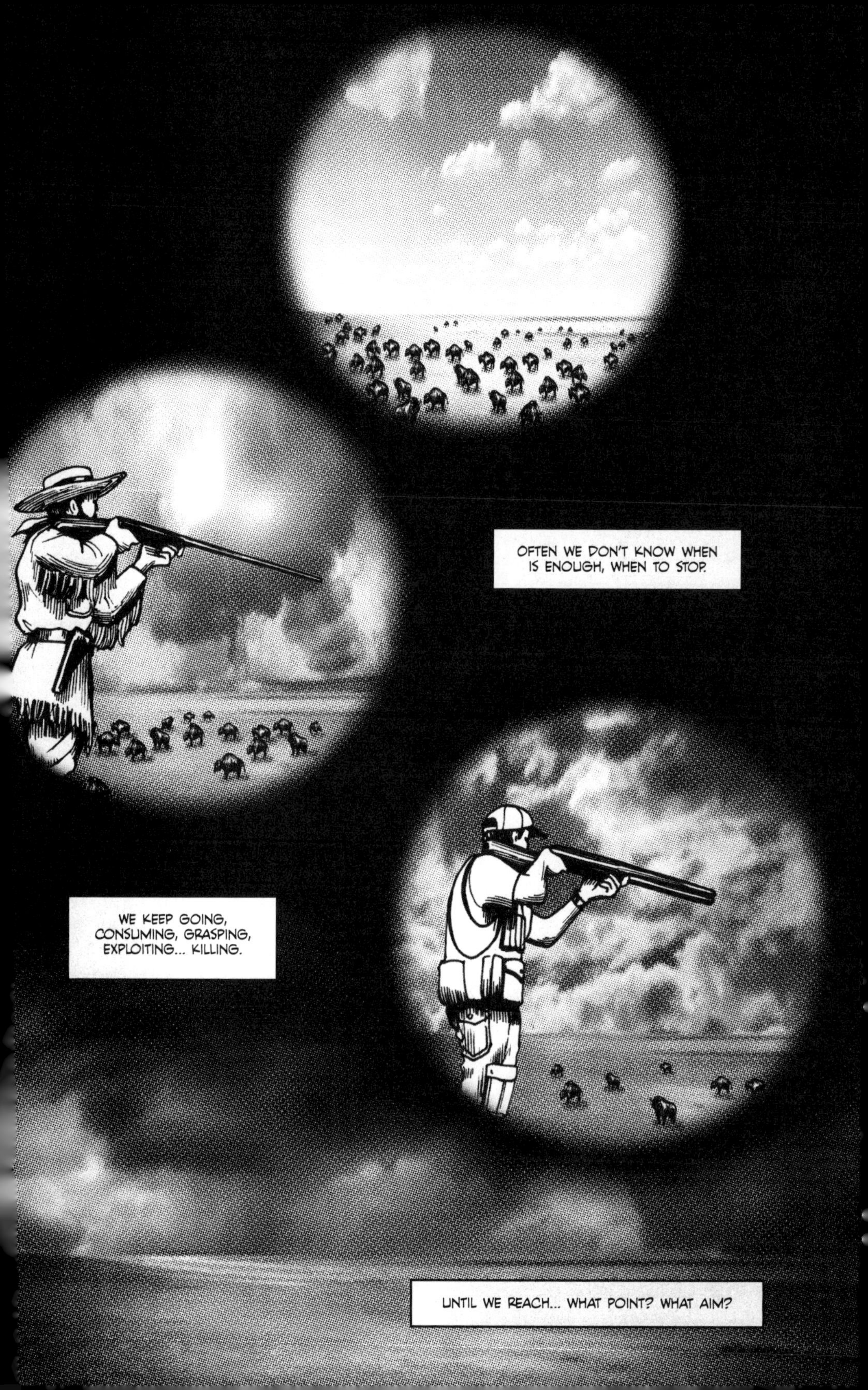
OFTEN WE DON'T KNOW WHEN IS ENOUGH, WHEN TO STOP.
WE KEEP GOING, CONSUMING, GRASPING, EXPLOITING... KILLING.
UNTIL WE REACH... WHAT POINT? WHAT AIM?

# 47

Know the world without leaving your door;

Observe heaven's Way without peering through your window.

When you go out and travel farther and farther away,

What you know for certain diminishes.

Therefore the sage

Does not step out, but knows with certainty;

Does not look around, but identifies things;

Does not fabricate, but things come to fruition.

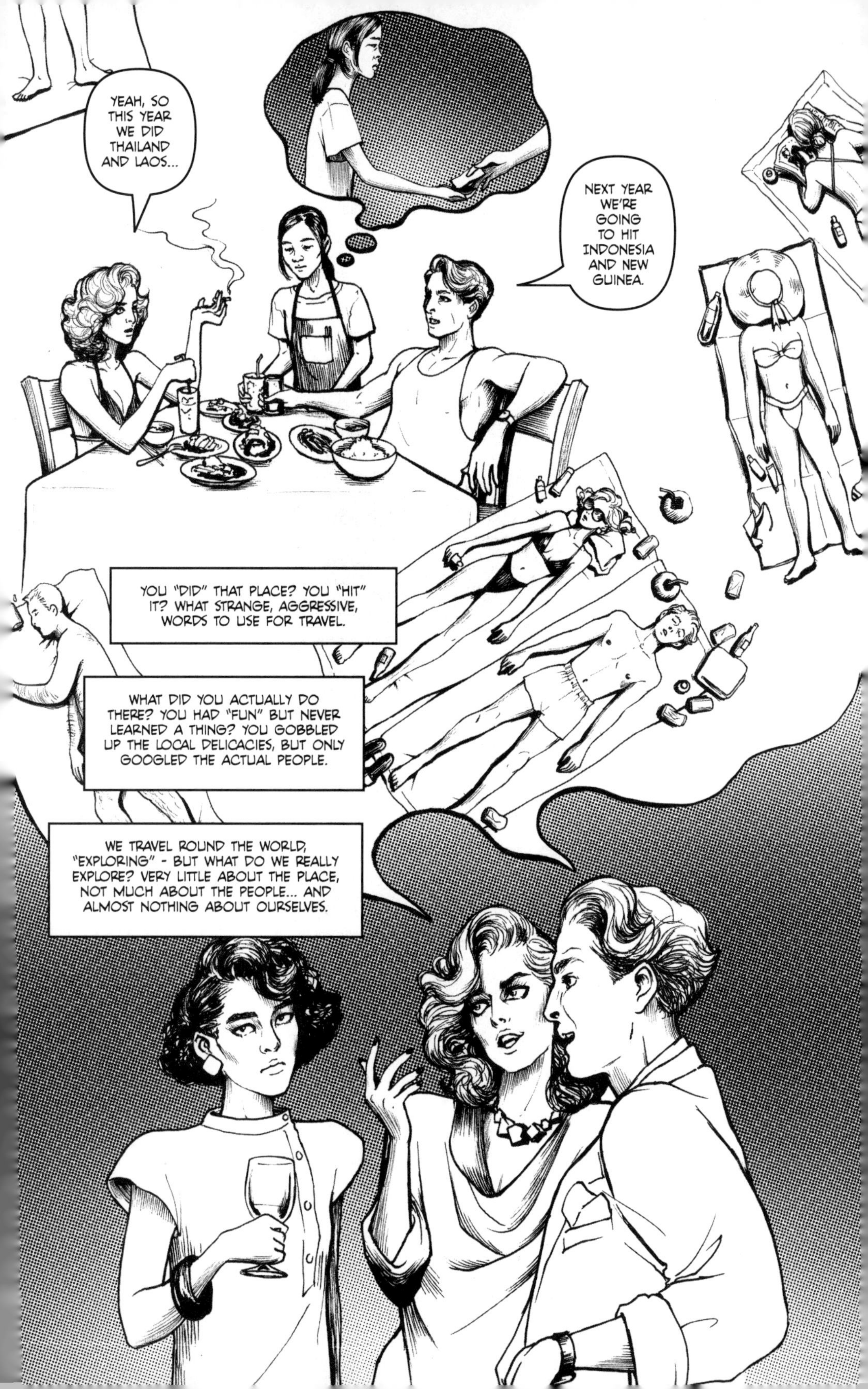
YEAH, SO THIS YEAR WE DID THAILAND AND LAOS...
NEXT YEAR WE'RE GOING TO HIT INDONESIA AND NEW GUINEA.
YOU "DID" THAT PLACE? YOU "HIT" IT? WHAT STRANGE, AGGRESSIVE, WORDS TO USE FOR TRAVEL.
WHAT DID YOU ACTUALLY DO THERE? YOU HAD "FUN" BUT NEVER LEARNED A THING? YOU GOBBLED UP THE LOCAL DELICACIES, BUT ONLY GOOGLED THE ACTUAL PEOPLE.
WE TRAVEL ROUND THE WORLD, "EXPLORING" - BUT WHAT DO WE REALLY EXPLORE? VERY LITTLE ABOUT THE PLACE, NOT MUCH ABOUT THE PEOPLE... AND ALMOST NOTHING ABOUT OURSELVES.

# 48

---

If you take up studying, you increase day by day.

If you take up the Way, you decrease day by day.

You decrease and then decrease again.

In this way, you reach the point of nonfabrication:

Nothing is fabricated, but there is nothing left undone.

Taking up the affairs of the world

Is always done without meddling.

If there is meddling,

It will not be sufficient to accomplish the job.

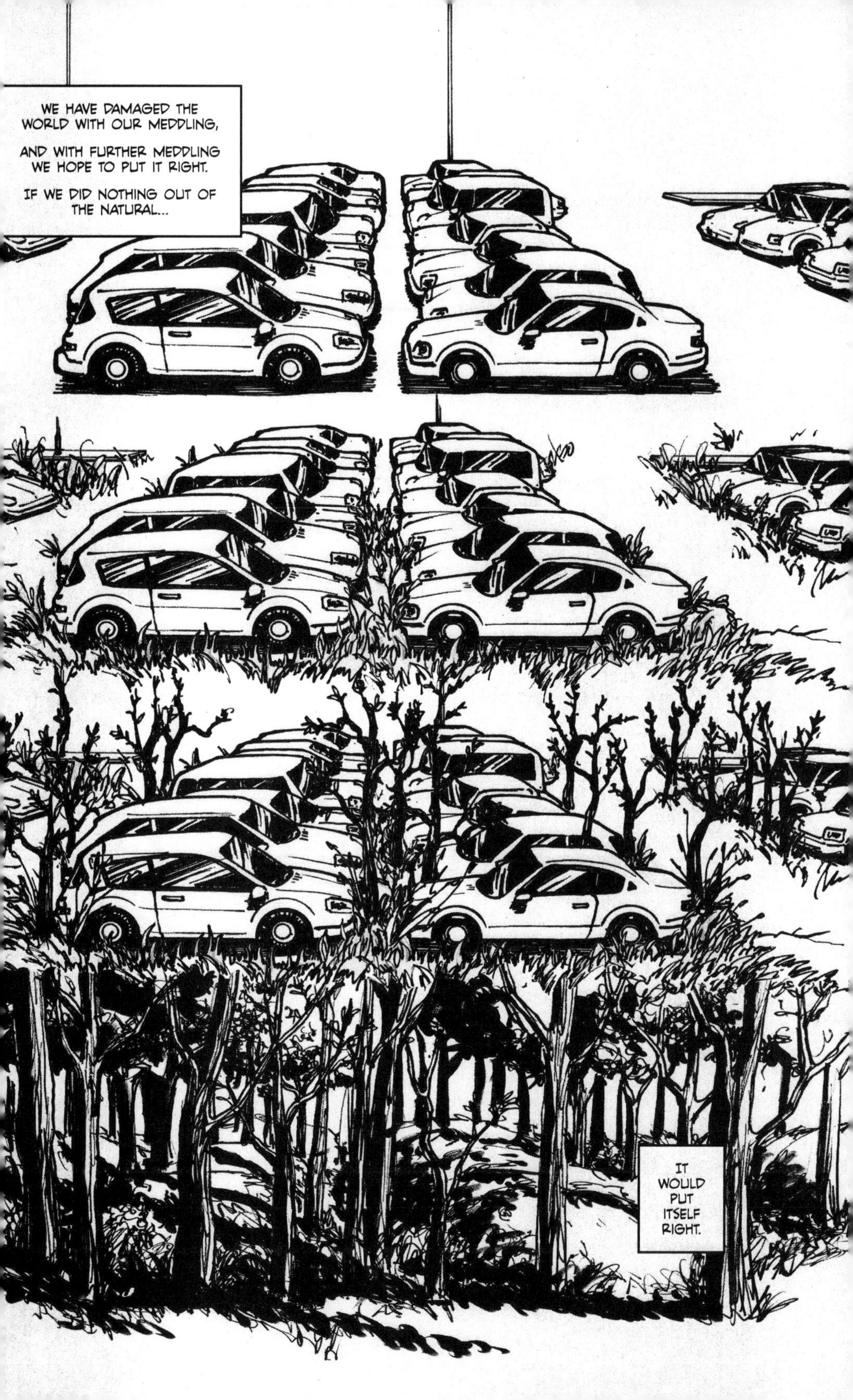
WE HAVE DAMAGED THE WORLD WITH OUR MEDDLING,
AND WITH FURTHER MEDDLING WE HOPE TO PUT IT RIGHT.
IF WE DID NOTHING OUT OF THE NATURAL...
IT WOULD PUT ITSELF RIGHT.

# 49

The sage does not have an unchanging mind.

He makes the mind of the people his own.

He is good to those who are good,

And good to those who are not good.

Thus, his virtue is good.

He stands by his words to those who stand by their words,

And he stands by his words to those who do not.

Thus, his virtue is reliable.

The sage resides in the world,

Harmonizes with it, and for the sake of the world, flows in convergence with its heartbeat.

People all give him their eyes and their ears,

And he treats them as he would laughing children.

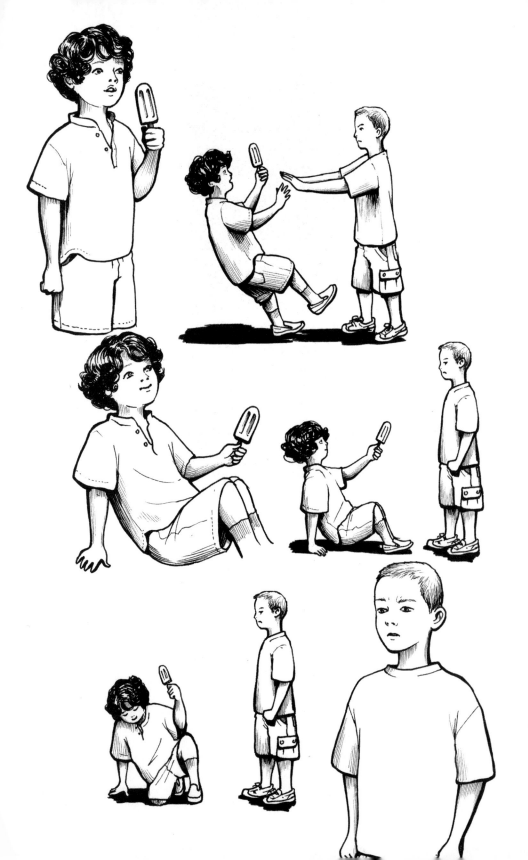

# 50

We come out into life, and go back into death.

Three out of ten follow along after life;

Three out of ten follow along after death;

And another three out of ten are given life, but by their activities march off after death.

Listen, why should this be?

It is because they are too strongly attached to life.

I have heard it generally said that a man who is good at taking care of his life

Will travel hill and dale, but not encounter wild horned buffalos or tigers;

He will enter a battlefield, but not put on protective armor.

The wild buffalo finds no place to thrust its horns,

The tiger finds no place to sink its claws,

And soldiers find no place to strike with their blades.

Now listen, why is this?

It is because for him, there is no dangerous place.

NOTHING HOLDS HIM,
DOOR AND WINDOWS OPEN,
TERRACES BROAD AND EMPTY.
STREET AND FIELD UNFOLDS BEFORE HIM,
ONTO DISTANT HILLS.

RIDGES AND TREES FALL UNDER HIM,
BEASTS AND BIRDS BEFRIEND HIM,
ALL THINGS CALM AT HIS PASSING.

WHATEVER HE TOUCHES
BECOMES A PLACID TIGER.
FOR HIM WITHOUT ENEMY,
THERE IS NO DANGER.

# 51

The Way gives them life.

Virtue gives them sustenance.

Color and shape give them form.

Energy gives them completion.

Therefore, the Ten Thousand Things

Respect the Way and treasure virtue.

Respecting the Way and treasuring virtue:

No one commands them to do this;

It is always just Of-Itself-So.

Thus, the Way gives them life,

And virtue gives them sustenance.

Both give them long life, and raise them as though
bringing them through childbirth.

Both give them refuge, and keep them from harm;

Both nourish them and provide them with cover;

Both give them life, but do not possess them.

Both act, but rely on nothing;

Both give them long life, but do not direct their affairs.

Both are called the dark and but dimly seen virtue.

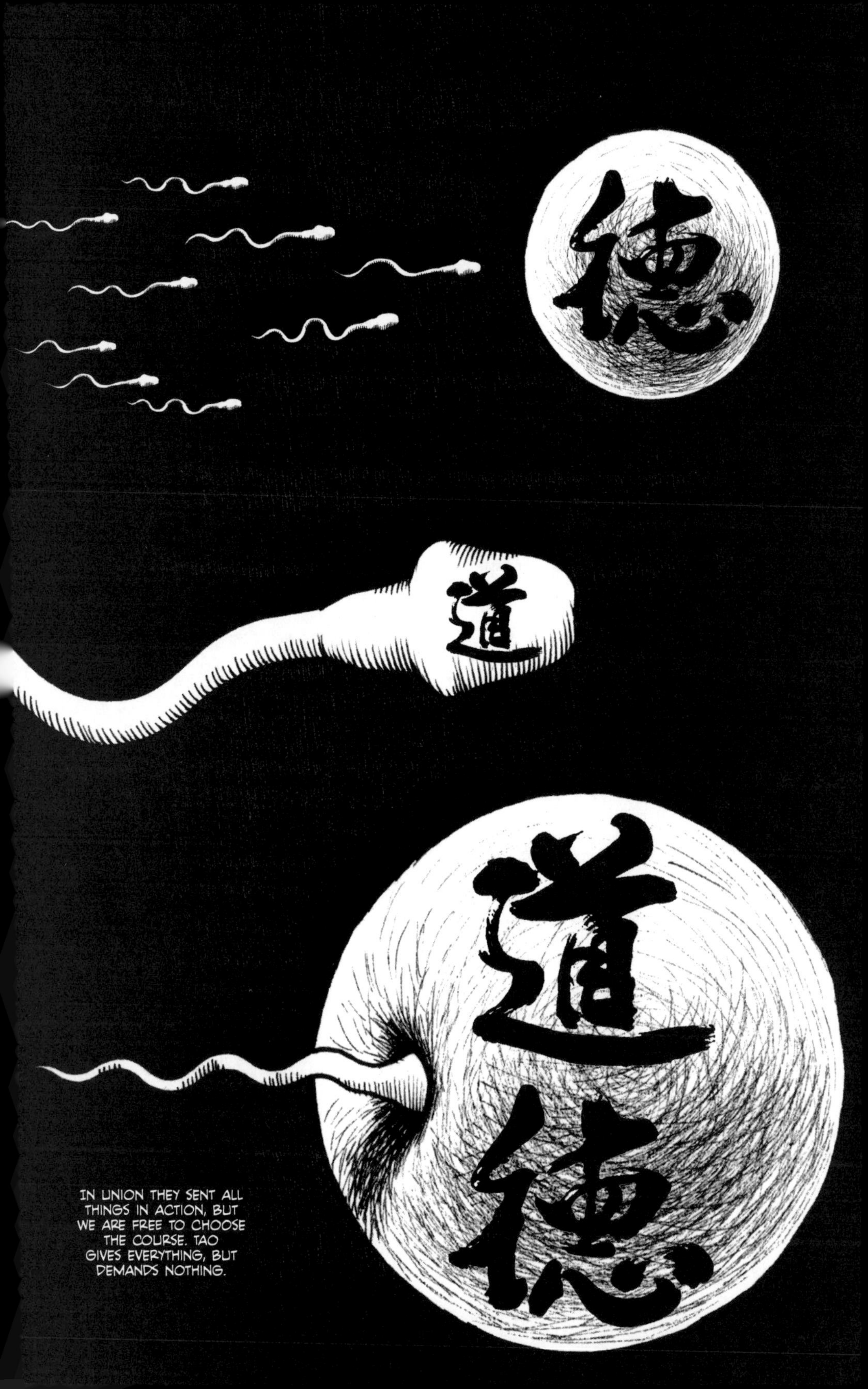
德
道
道德
IN UNION THEY SENT ALL THINGS IN ACTION, BUT WE ARE FREE TO CHOOSE THE COURSE. TAO GIVES EVERYTHING, BUT DEMANDS NOTHING.

# 52

All beneath heaven has a beginning;

You could consider it the nursing mother of the world.

When you have grasped who that mother is,

You will also clearly know who her children are.

When you clearly know who the children are,

You will, in turn, sustain the mother.

Thus, you will not be in danger to your very last gasp.

Plug up the leaks as you would a wall with mud,

Close up the gates with a bar,

And to the end of your life you will not feel the squeeze of your endeavors.

Open up the leaks,

Let them go to work,

And to the end of your life, nothing will be of any help.

Observing the infinitesimal is called the illumination of the sun and moon;

Maintaining the soft and malleable is called the strength of the wasp's sting.

If you make use of a light as intense as a fire

And return again to its illumination,

Life's disasters will be gone and forgotten.

This is called the practice of the Unchanging.

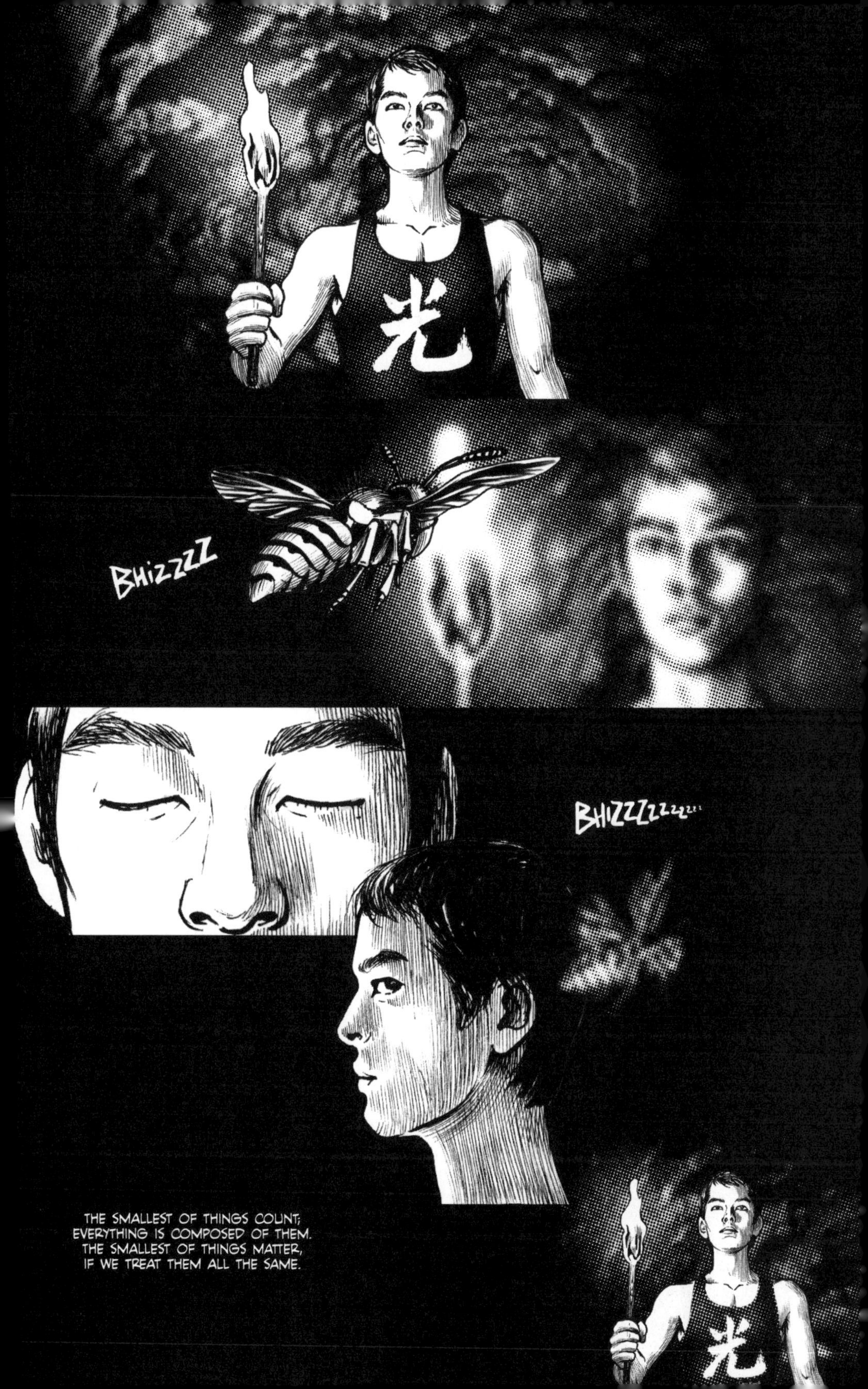
光
BHIZZZZ
BHIZZZZZZZZZ
THE SMALLEST OF THINGS COUNT;
EVERYTHING IS COMPOSED OF THEM.
THE SMALLEST OF THINGS MATTER,
IF WE TREAT THEM ALL THE SAME.
光

# 53

If I should allow myself even a small portion of
knowledge,

When putting one foot in front of the other on the
Great Way,

I fear that I would only wander off a twisting bypath.

The Great Way is extraordinarily broad, like a bow
when drawn,

But the people favor narrow ways.

Though the courts are swept clean of honesty,

The fields are choked with reedy weeds,

And the warehouses are quite empty;

Beautifully patterned robes are worn,

Sharp swords are fastened to sashes,

Food and drink are consumed to surfeit,

And valuables and capital are at hand in excess.

This is called the grandeur of thieves.

It is emphatically not the Way.

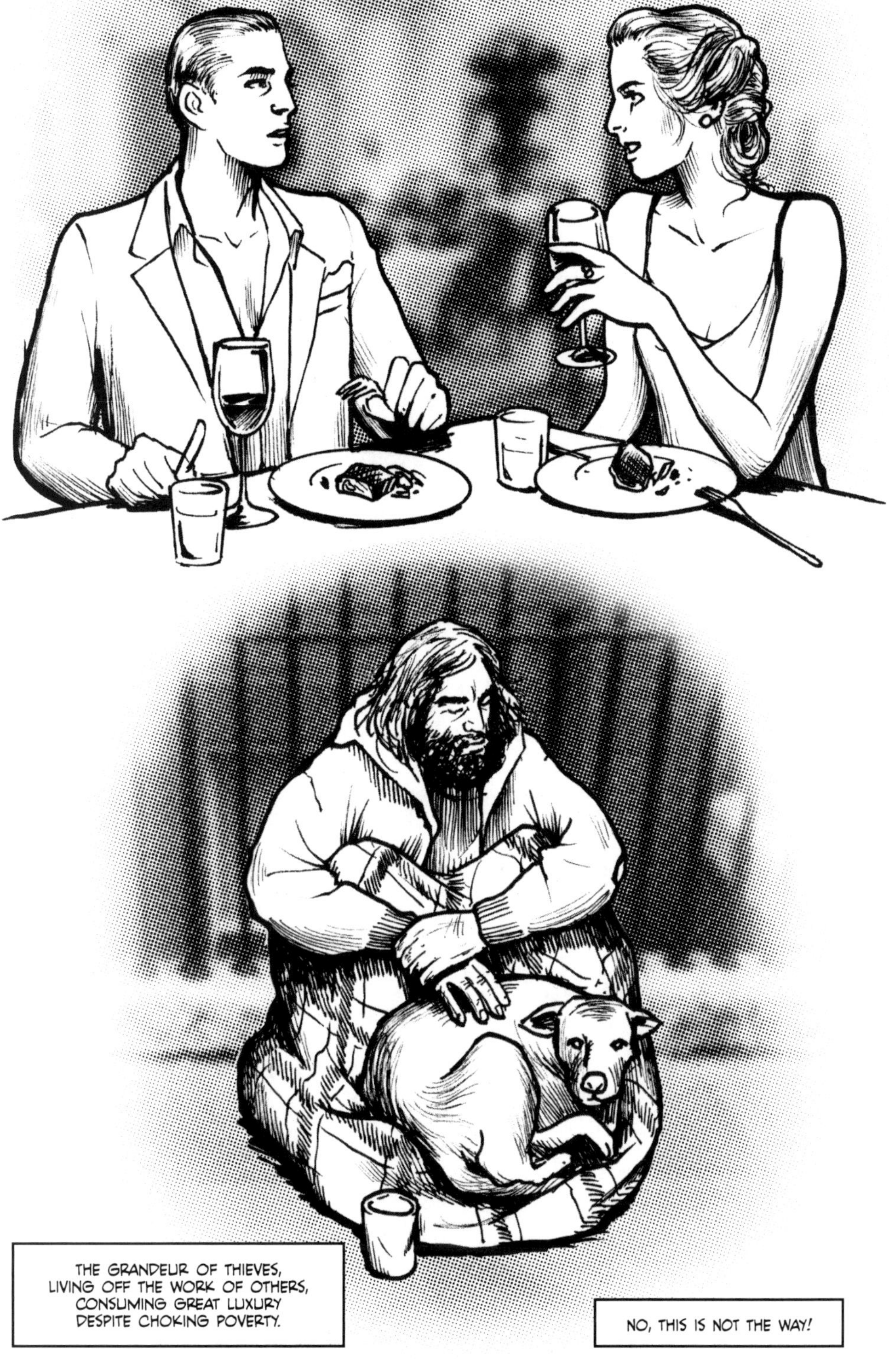
THE GRANDEUR OF THIEVES, LIVING OFF THE WORK OF OTHERS, CONSUMING GREAT LUXURY DESPITE CHOKING POVERTY.
NO, THIS IS NOT THE WAY!

# 54

He who is well set up, like a brush held erect, will not be pulled away.

He who embraces it with both hands, will not have it slip away;

Thus, his descendents will not pause in performing sacrifices to his spirit.

If you cultivate this for your own person as you would sweep and prune,

Its virtue will be pure.

If you cultivate this in the same way for your household,

Its virtue will be plentiful.

If you cultivate this among those in your village,

Its virtue will be long lasting.

If you cultivate this among those within your provincial borders,

Its virtue will be like vessels filled with an abundant harvest.

If you cultivate this with all under heaven,

Its virtue will go everywhere.

Thus, you should contemplate a household as a household,

You should contemplate those in a village as those in a village,

You should contemplate a country as a country.

And all under heaven will be contemplated as all under heaven.

How do I know that this is so for all under heaven?

I know from this very order of things.

# 55

He who holds on to virtue sincerely and deeply within

Can be compared to a newborn child.

Wasps, scorpions, vipers, and other snakes will not sting or bite him;

Fierce beasts will not reach for him with their claws;

And birds of prey will not strike him with curled talons.

His bones will be pliant, his sinews will be soft, and yet his grasp will be unyielding.

He does not yet know the conjoining of male and female parts, but his own stands right up.

His pure spirit has arrived like an arrow piercing the earth.

He may scream like a tiger the entire day, but his throat will not become parched.

His harmony, too, is at its best.

Knowing harmony is called the Unchanging;

Knowing the Unchanging is called illumination.

To make life overflow its limits is said to be bad luck in the guise of good.

For the mind to put *ch'i* at its beck and call is said to be forceful.

When creatures reach their peak, they become deformed and distorted.

This is said not to be following the Way.

Those who do not follow the Way, soon come to an end.

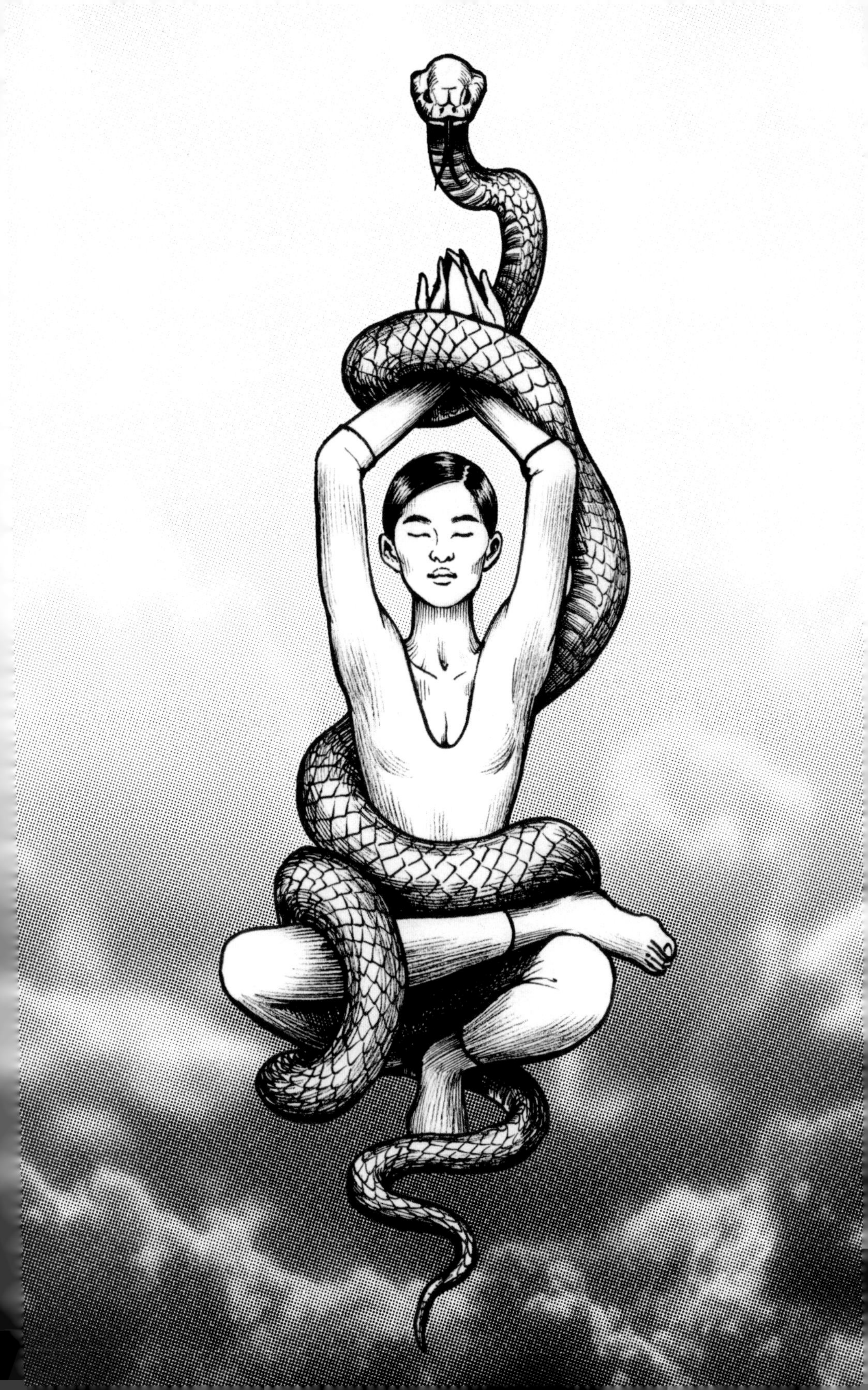

# 56

The knowing do not speak.

Those speaking do not know.

Plug up the leaks as you would a wall with mud,

Close up the gates with a bar.

Blunt your pointiness,

Unravel your tangles,

Soften your blazing light,

Become as the dust raised by a herd of passing deer.

This is called the dark identity.

With such a person, no family intimacy can be obtained,

But neither can distance or estrangement.

From him, advantage cannot be obtained,

But neither can hurt or harm.

He cannot be valued,

Nor considered of no account.

Thus he is treasured by all under heaven.

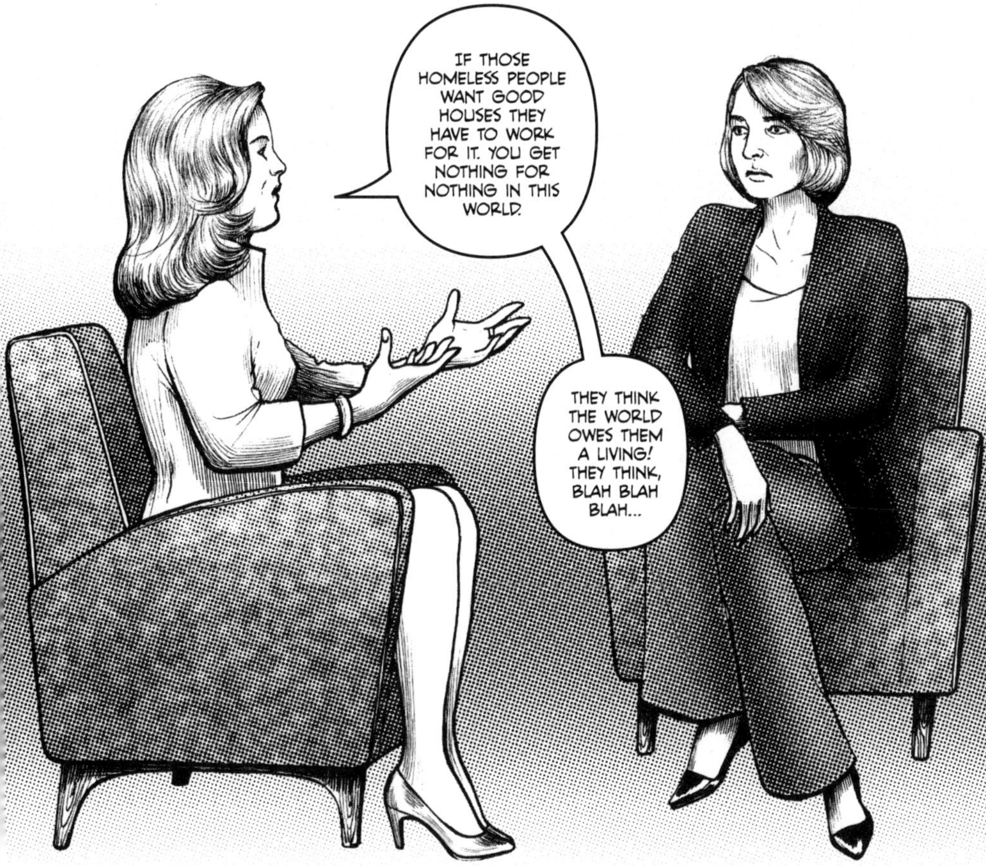
IF THOSE HOMELESS PEOPLE WANT GOOD HOUSES THEY HAVE TO WORK FOR IT. YOU GET NOTHING FOR NOTHING IN THIS WORLD.
THEY THINK THE WORLD OWES THEM A LIVING! THEY THINK, BLAH BLAH BLAH...
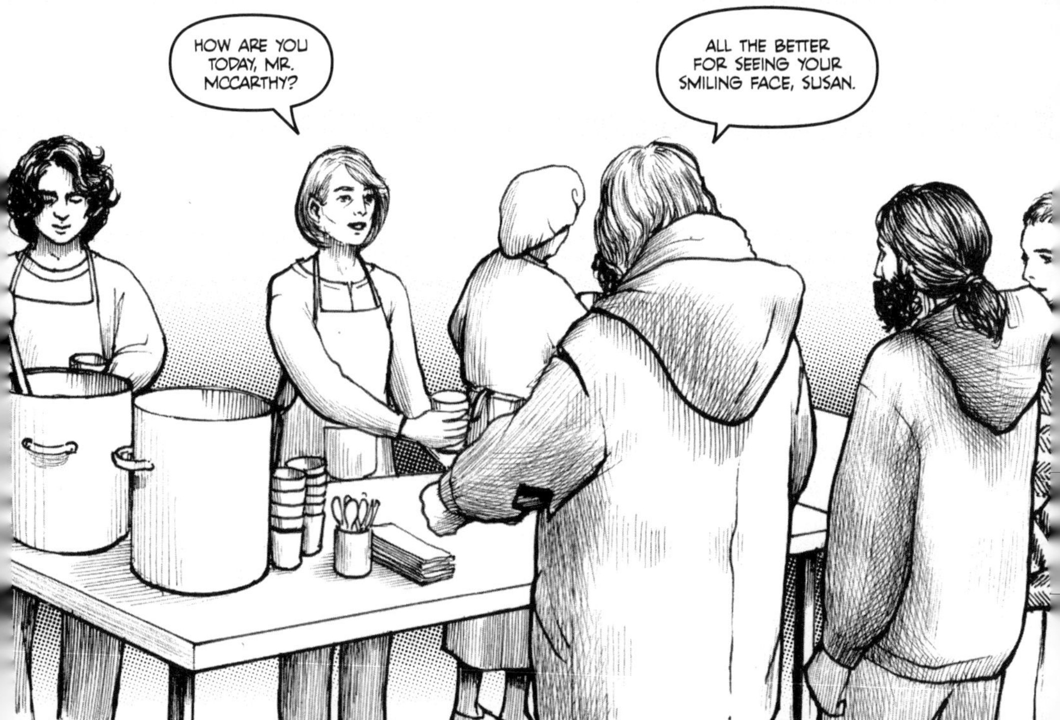
HOW ARE YOU TODAY, MR. MCCARTHY?
ALL THE BETTER FOR SEEING YOUR SMILING FACE, SUSAN.

# 57

Manage the flow of the state with impartiality;

Use the military in an unexpected manner;

Take the world as you would a trophy from a
vanquished foe without even putting your hand to it.

How do I know this can be so?

From this very order of things:

When fear and loathing proliferate in the world,

The people will become increasingly destitute.

When the people have an abundance of sharp weapons
and clever leaders,

The state will become increasingly dusky and dark.

When men are filled with stratagems and cunning,

Strange and eccentric objects will appear with
fecundity.

When laws and commands are drummed up time
and again,

More and more burglars and muggers will be at hand.

Thus, the sage says,

> I do nothing creative, and the people change of
> themselves;

> I am fond of restraint in conflict, and the people
> become impartial on their own;

> I put my hand to nothing, and the people prosper
> by themselves;

> I desire nothing, and the people have unvarnished
> simplicity on their own.

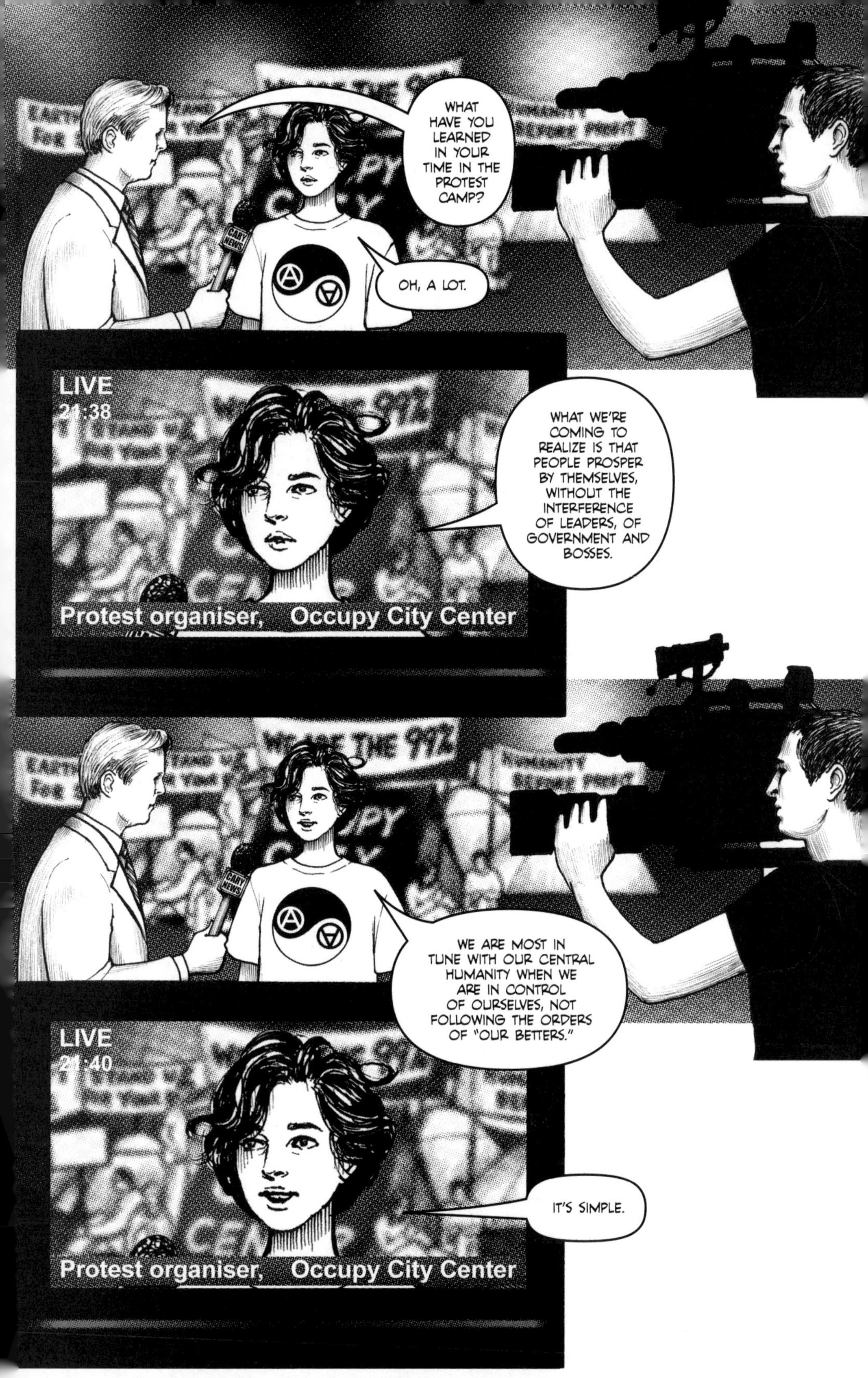

WHAT HAVE YOU LEARNED IN YOUR TIME IN THE PROTEST CAMP?
OH, A LOT.
LIVE
21:38
WHAT WE'RE COMING TO REALIZE IS THAT PEOPLE PROSPER BY THEMSELVES, WITHOUT THE INTERFERENCE OF LEADERS, OF GOVERNMENT AND BOSSES.
Protest organiser, Occupy City Center
WE ARE MOST IN TUNE WITH OUR CENTRAL HUMANITY WHEN WE ARE IN CONTROL OF OURSELVES, NOT FOLLOWING THE ORDERS OF "OUR BETTERS."
LIVE
21:40
IT'S SIMPLE.
Protest organiser, Occupy City Center

# 58

If the affairs of the state are gloomy and troubled,

The people will be confined like water unable to flow;

Yet when the affairs of state are clear and exacting,

The people will find themselves lacking.

Disaster hinges on good fortune,

While blessings from the gods lie concealed within distorted circumstances.

Who knows when either reaches its limit?

There is nothing that does not eventually lean one way or the other.

Correctness again creates eccentricity;

Good again creates the suspicious.

Men have no clear vision of their way,

As has been since days long ago.

For this reason, the sage

Is four-cornered, but does not cut with sharp edges;

Is a sharp straight crease, but does not tear;

Has straightened what was once bent, but does not stretch things out self-indulgently;

Is as bright as a blazing fire, but does not flash or flare.

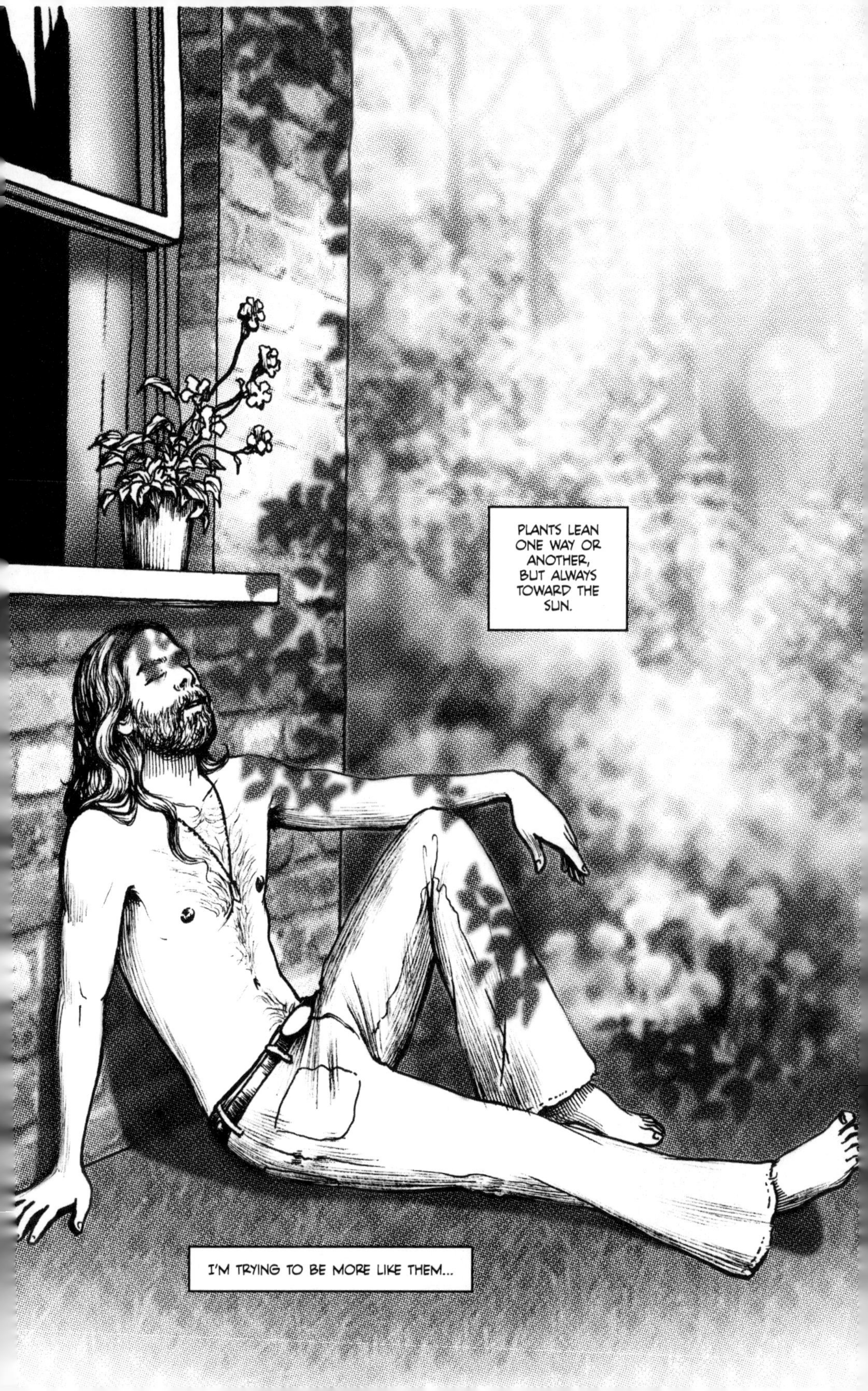
PLANTS LEAN ONE WAY OR ANOTHER, BUT ALWAYS TOWARD THE SUN.
I'M TRYING TO BE MORE LIKE THEM...

# 59

For directing the flow of human affairs, and offering your hand to heaven's,

There is nothing like frugality, as you would put grain carefully away in a storehouse.

Listen, only such frugality

Is said to be quick obeisance to the Way.

Quick obeisance is said to accumulate virtue, layer upon layer.

Accumulating virtue in this way is exactly like donning a helmet and becoming unbeatable.

Being unbeatable,

You will know no limits.

Knowing no limits,

You will have the country in your hand.

Having the nursing mother of the country in your hands,

You will last long into old age, with long white hair and a cane.

This is called having deep roots and strong radicles.

It is the Way of long life and unwavering vision.

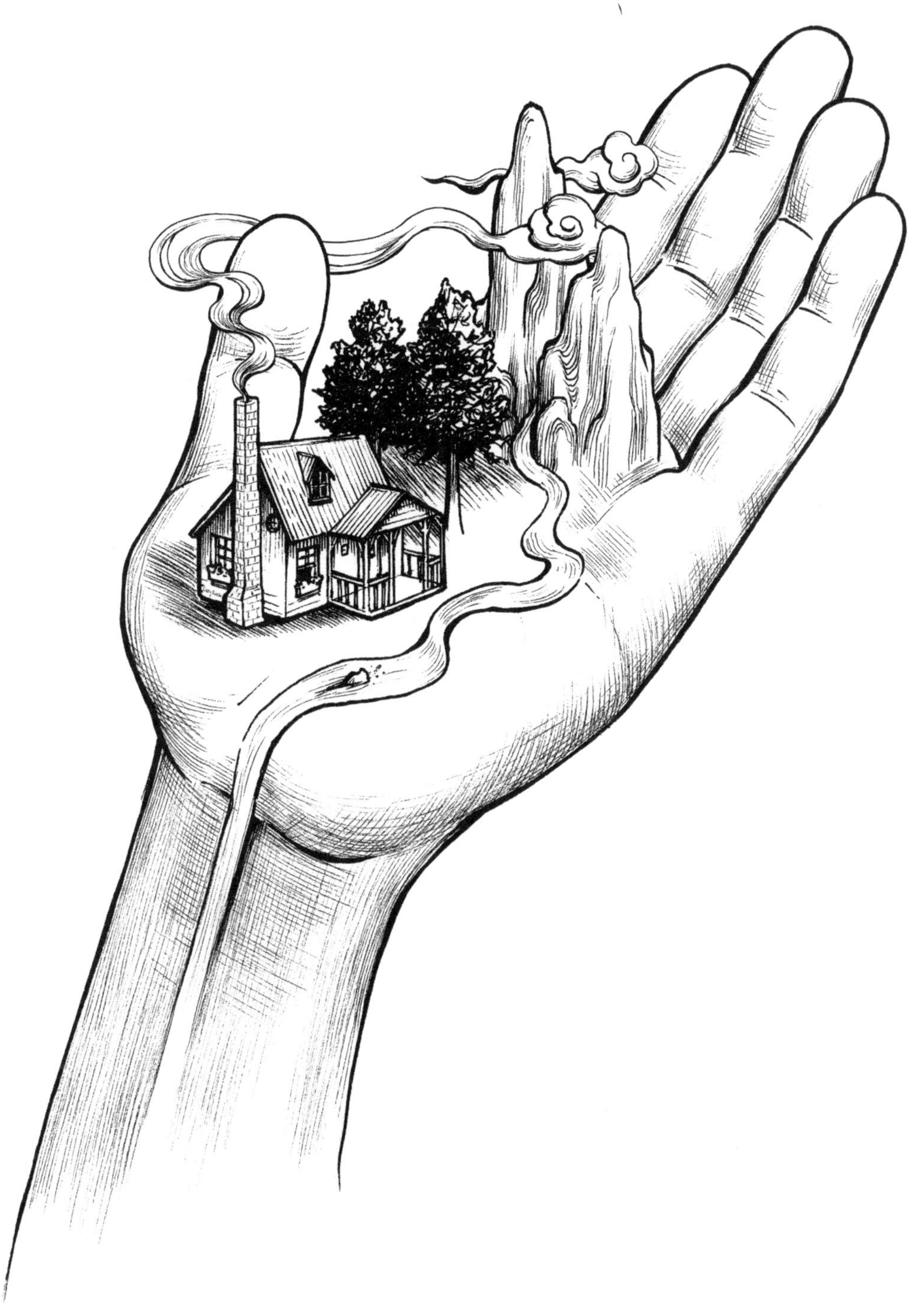

# 60

Directing the flow of affairs of a large country

Is like cooking a small fresh fish.


When going out and confronting the world with
the Way

The gods and demons are no longer like thunder and
lightning.

And it's not just that they're no longer like thunder and
lightning,

But they can no longer harm people with their slings
and arrows.

And it's not just that they can no longer harm people
with their slings and arrows,

But the sage cannot harm them in like way either.


Listen, when none of these can do harm this way,

Virtues return home one after another.

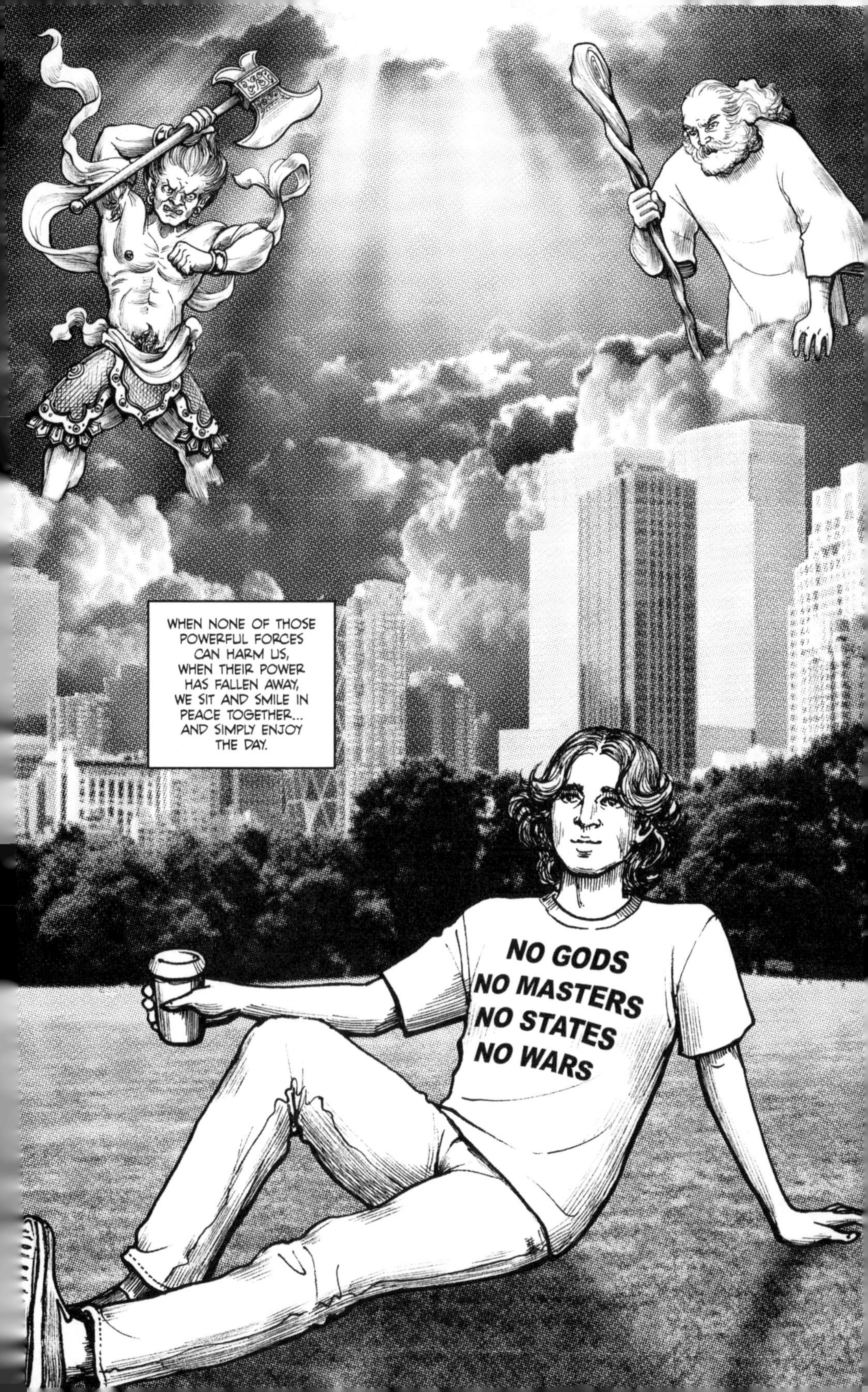
WHEN NONE OF THOSE POWERFUL FORCES CAN HARM US, WHEN THEIR POWER HAS FALLEN AWAY, WE SIT AND SMILE IN PEACE TOGETHER... AND SIMPLY ENJOY THE DAY.
NO GODS
NO MASTERS
NO STATES
NO WARS

# 61

A large country resembles the lower reaches of a river:

Here, all under heaven meet and mix like the alternate collars of a robe,

And this is the female of the world.

The female constantly overcomes the male by means of peace and noncontention;

With peace and noncontention, it takes the lower position.

Thus, if a large country places itself in a lower position than a small country,

It will take that small country like a victor in war takes the left ear of the vanquished as a trophy.

If a small country takes a position beneath a large country,

It will take that large country in the same way.

Thus, there are cases when you may take others by putting yourself in the lower position,

And cases when you may take others by having been in the lower position in the first place.

Large countries do not go beyond wanting to unite men in one political entity and to lay them in stock as they might grains from the fields.

Small countries want nothing more than to enter into the service of large countries.

Listen, if both get what they desire,

The large country should happily put itself in the lower position.

# 62

The Way is the storehouse and kitchen of the Ten
Thousand Things.

It is a treasure for the good man who is a blessing
for all,

And a place of support for the bad man, as it would
carry him on its back as though he were a child.

Beautiful words can bring you respect in the
marketplace;

Beautiful behavior can bring men to your side.

As for a man with nothing good about him,

Would you throw him away like tossing out trash with
both hands?

Thus, when a new emperor is established,

When the Three Ministers are set in place,

Though you may offer up large, elaborately decorated
pieces of jade with both hands, and precede these with
chariots drawn by four horses,

This is nothing like kneeling in the dirt and proposing
the Way.

Why did the men of old treasure this Way?

Didn't they say that those who seek it out will pick it up
along the way,

And that those who have been caught like fish in the
nets of crime will be pardoned and given new life?

Thus, it makes all under heaven treasure it.

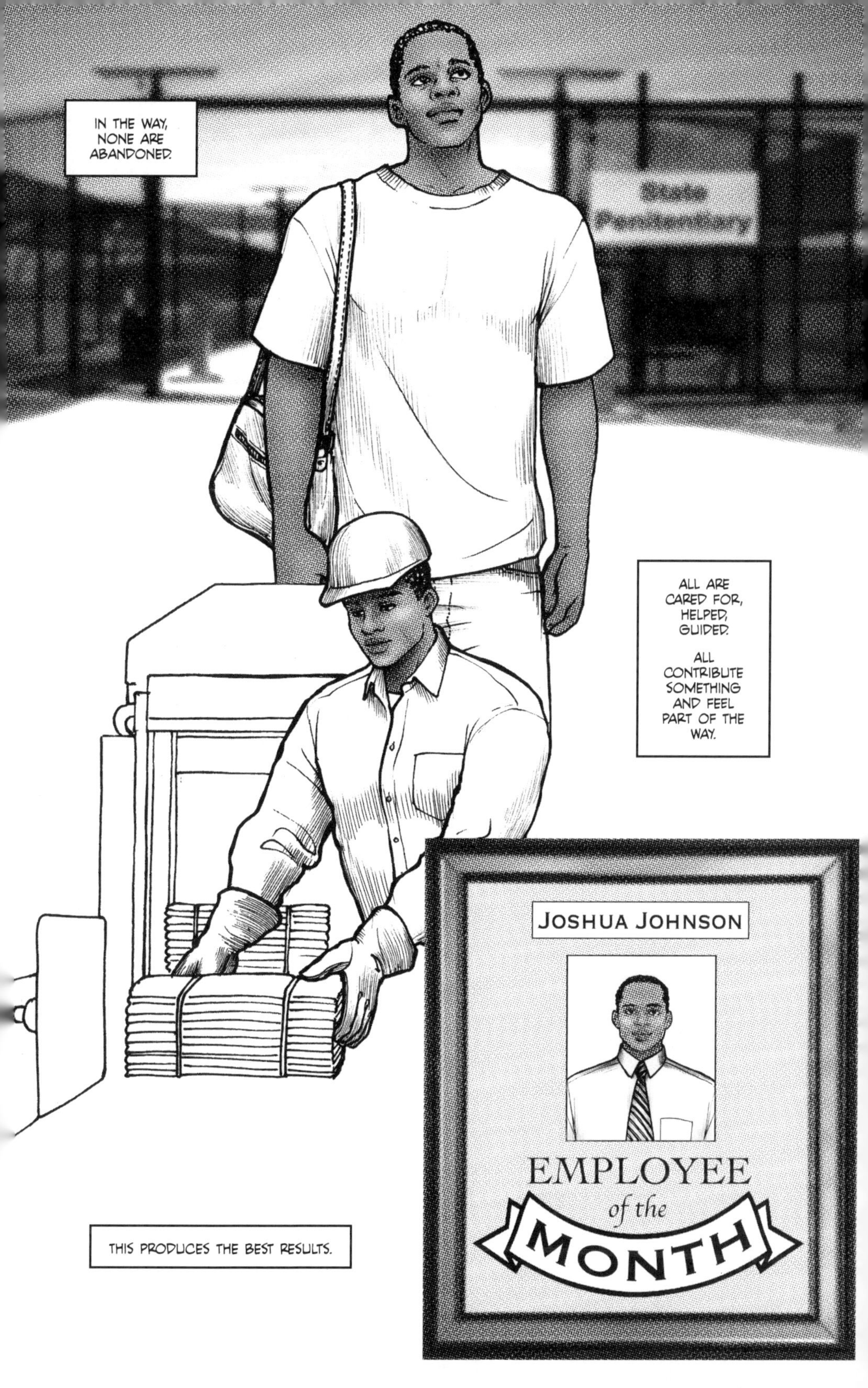
IN THE WAY, NONE ARE ABANDONED.
ALL ARE CARED FOR, HELPED, GUIDED.
ALL CONTRIBUTE SOMETHING AND FEEL PART OF THE WAY.
THIS PRODUCES THE BEST RESULTS.
JOSHUA JOHNSON
EMPLOYEE of the MONTH

# 63

Act without fabrication.

Do the job without putting your hand to it.

Experience the delicious without tasting.

Large, small, many, few—

Return another's spitefully turning his back on you
with virtue.

Map out a plan for the difficult while it is yet easy to
change, like a chameleon's colors.

Do something with the big, while it is still small and
vaguely formed.

The difficult things in the world are invariably fashioned
from the easy.

The great affairs under heaven are invariably fashioned
from the small.

Therefore the sage,

In the end, does not work on the large.

Thus, the large becomes realized.

Listen, there are few who will stand by their words
after lightly giving assent.

What appears to be too easy will invariably be too
difficult.

Therefore the sage has doubts and gets ready for
difficulties.

Thus, in the end, there are no difficulties at all.

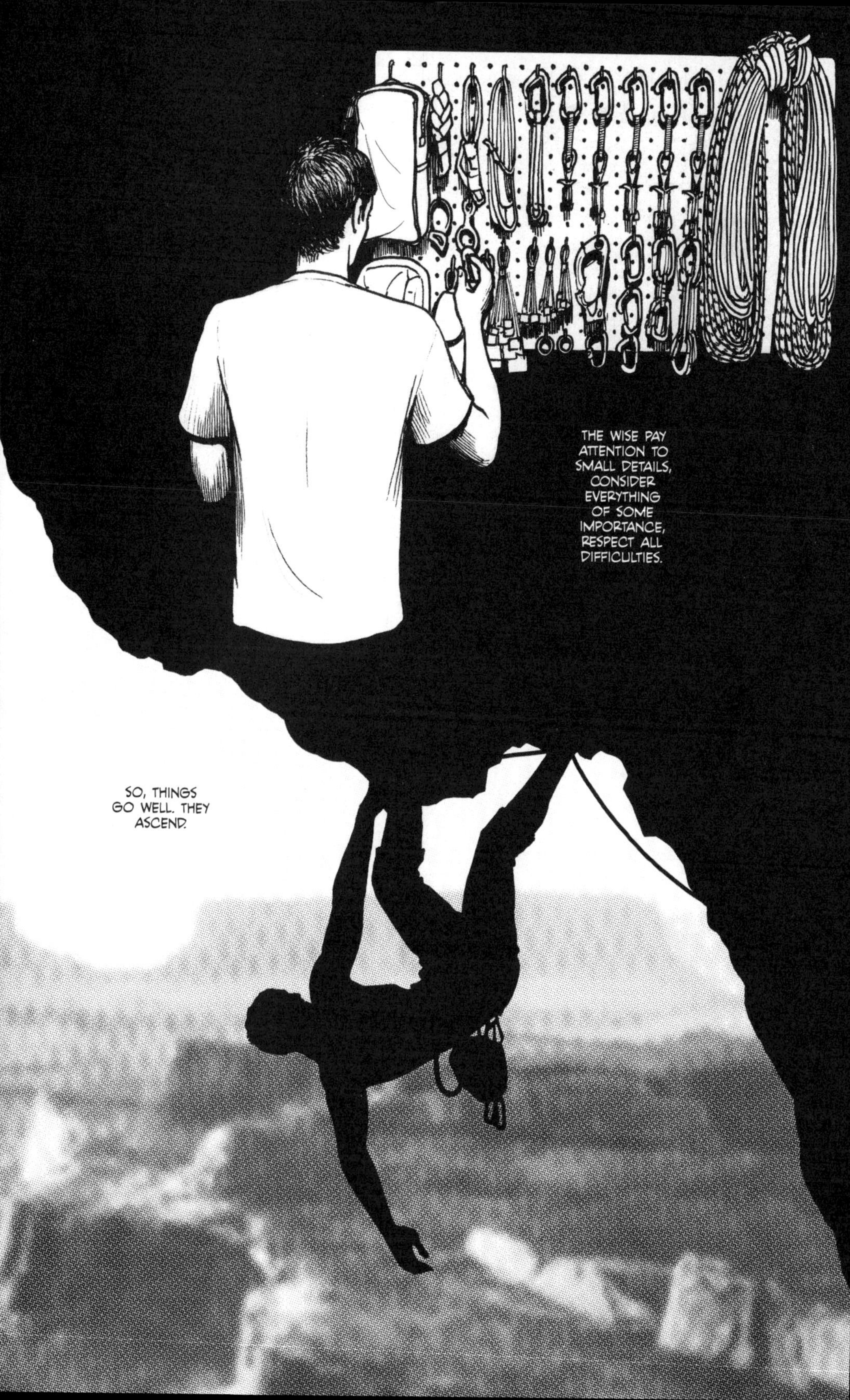
THE WISE PAY ATTENTION TO SMALL DETAILS, CONSIDER EVERYTHING OF SOME IMPORTANCE, RESPECT ALL DIFFICULTIES.
SO, THINGS GO WELL. THEY ASCEND.

# 64

That which is settled and calm is easy to hold in
your hands.

That which has not yet manifested omens or signs
is easy to plan for with no one the wiser.

That which is fragile is easy to crack.

That still in bits and pieces is easy to scatter like chips
of bamboo.

Take care of things while they are not yet at hand.

Manage the flow of things while they are not yet in
disarray.


A tree big enough to put your arms around

Sprouts from a seedling as fine as a hair.

A tower of nine stories

Goes bottom to top from continuous piles of earth.

A walk of a thousand *li*

Begins beneath your feet.

He who acts on something, breaks it.

He who fetters something, loses it.

For this reason, the sage

    Does not fabricate, and thus breaks nothing;

    Does not fetter, and thus loses nothing.

People follow along with their affairs,

Which unfailingly collapse as completion nears.

If they were as sincere in the end as they were in the beginning,

There would be no collapsing at all.

Therefore the sage

> Desires to have no desires,

> And does not treasure capital difficult to obtain.

> He studies how not to study,

> And turns back where many men go too far.

In this way he assists the Ten Thousand Things to be Of-Themselves-So,

But is not eager to concoct anything himself.

# 65

The men of old who did well with the Way

Did not thereby illuminate the people.

Rather, they used it to keep them thinking in circles.

The current affairs of the people are difficult to manage

Because they have too much "wisdom."

Thus, using "wisdom" to manage the flow of the state

Is piracy of the state.

Managing the flow of the state without this kind of wisdom

Is the state's good fortune.


He who understands these two clearly

Has understood the law of where to stop with thought.

Constant knowledge of this law

Is called the dark and mysterious virtue.

The dark and mysterious virtue runs so deep, so distant!

With it, all creatures return.

In this way—stepping back—they arrive at the great order of things.

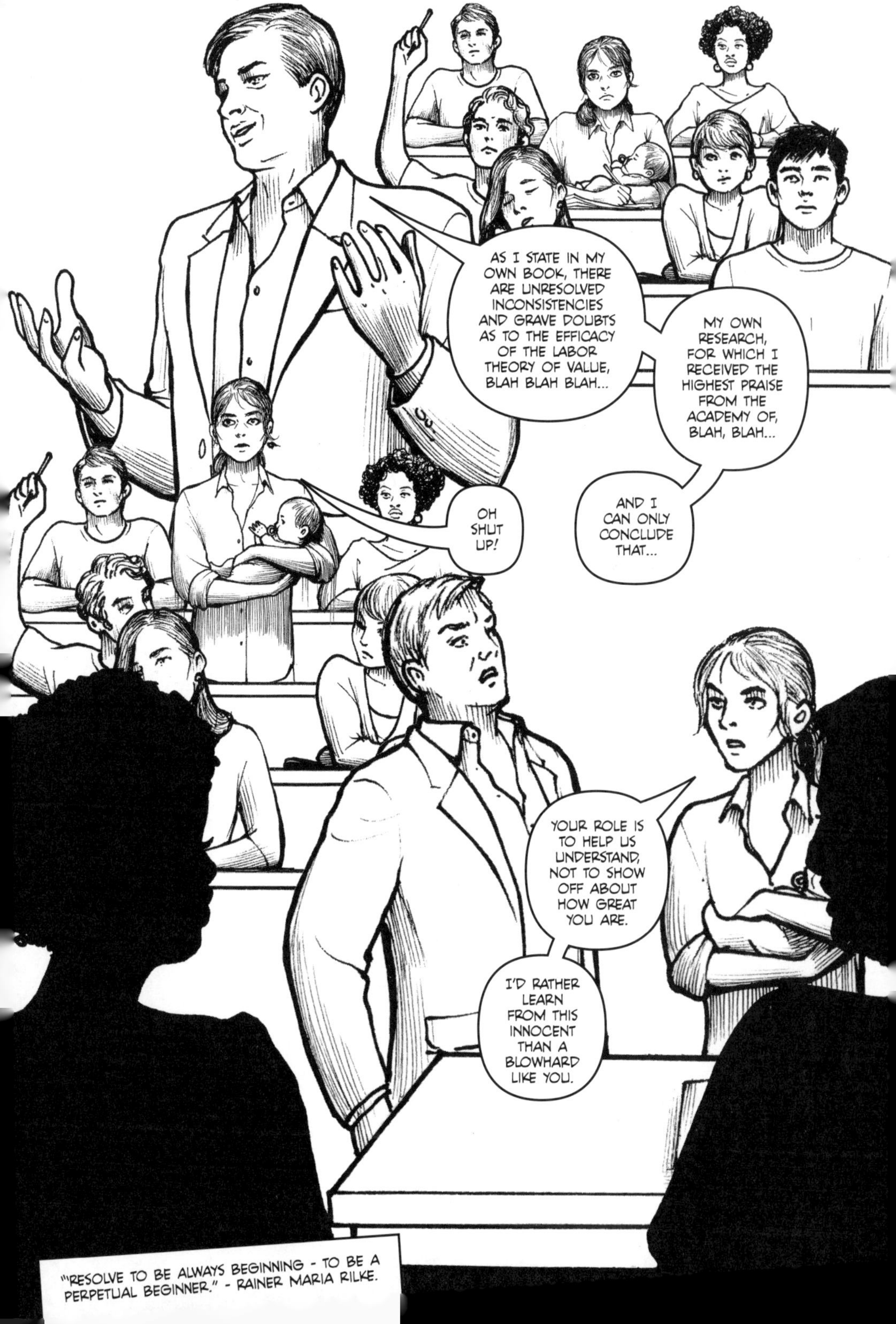
AS I STATE IN MY OWN BOOK, THERE ARE UNRESOLVED INCONSISTENCIES AND GRAVE DOUBTS AS TO THE EFFICACY OF THE LABOR THEORY OF VALUE, BLAH BLAH BLAH...
MY OWN RESEARCH, FOR WHICH I RECEIVED THE HIGHEST PRAISE FROM THE ACADEMY OF, BLAH, BLAH...
AND I CAN ONLY CONCLUDE THAT...
OH SHUT UP!
YOUR ROLE IS TO HELP US UNDERSTAND, NOT TO SHOW OFF ABOUT HOW GREAT YOU ARE.
I'D RATHER LEARN FROM THIS INNOCENT THAN A BLOWHARD LIKE YOU.
"RESOLVE TO BE ALWAYS BEGINNING - TO BE A PERPETUAL BEGINNER." - RAINER MARIA RILKE.

# 66

There is a reason why the great flowing rivers and the ocean can make themselves kings of the myriad mountain streams:

It is because they are well below them.

Thus, they are able to make themselves kings of the myriad mountain streams.

For this reason, if you wish to be above the people,

You must invariably say that you are below them.

If you wish to be ahead of the people,

You must invariably place yourself to follow them up from behind.

For this reason, the sage

> Takes his place above, but the people do not feel him to be heavy baggage;

> Takes his place in front, but the people do not consider him an obstruction.

For this reason, all under heaven enjoy reverencing him, but never feel cramped or importuned.

It is because he does not contend with others

That none under heaven can contend with him.

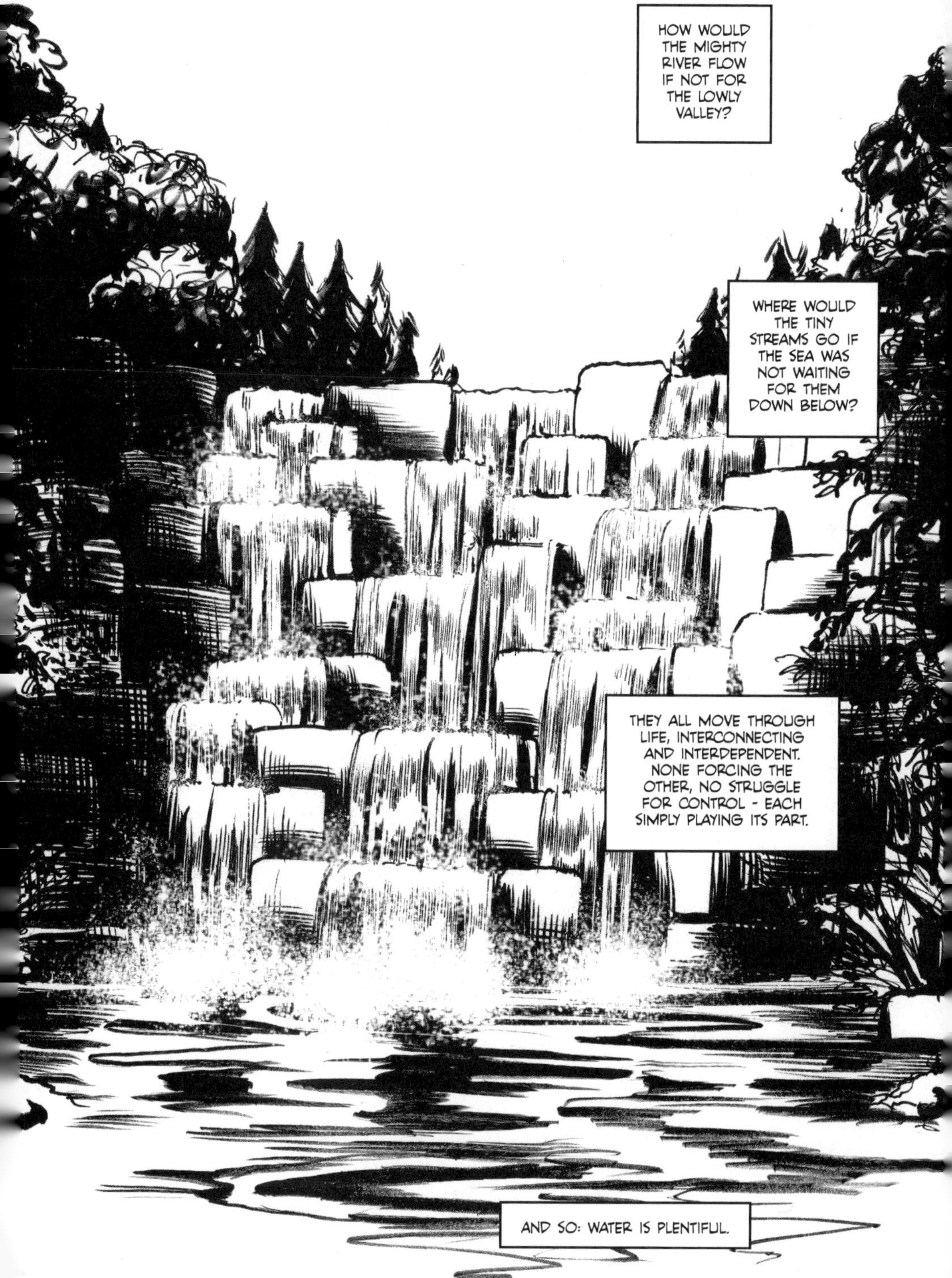
HOW WOULD THE MIGHTY RIVER FLOW IF NOT FOR THE LOWLY VALLEY?
WHERE WOULD THE TINY STREAMS GO IF THE SEA WAS NOT WAITING FOR THEM DOWN BELOW?
THEY ALL MOVE THROUGH LIFE, INTERCONNECTING AND INTERDEPENDENT. NONE FORCING THE OTHER, NO STRUGGLE FOR CONTROL - EACH SIMPLY PLAYING ITS PART.
AND SO: WATER IS PLENTIFUL.

# 67

All under heaven declare that my Way is great, but it resembles something less worthy.

Listen, it's only great

Because it doesn't look that way.

If it had such a resemblance,

How faint it would have been, and for so long!

I myself have three treasures at hand;

I keep a firm grasp on them, and protect them as I would a child carried on my back.

The first, I say, is nurturing love.

The second, I say, is unpretentiousness.

The third, I say, is not pushing myself ahead in the world.

Because of nurturing love, you are capable of courage that flows forth;

Because of unpretentiousness, you are capable of being expansive;

Because of not pushing yourself ahead in the world,

You are capable of having the stature of an elder among people of ability.

If you put nurturing love aside, and would still have gushing courage;

If you put unpretentiousness aside, and would still be expansive;

If you put following along behind aside, and would still be in the fore;

You will turn to white bones and desiccated flesh.

Listen, with nurturing love,

If you are brought into conflict, you will overcome the opposition.

If you will maintain this love, you will be firm.

When heaven is going to intervene,

It protects you unexpectedly with nurturing love.

# 68

The man who makes himself a good warrior does not stride fiercely forward with a spear.

The man good in battle will repress all anger.

The man good at defeating his opponent will not clash with him directly.

The man good at using others will put himself in a low position.

This is said to be the virtue of noncontending.

It is said to be the use of other men's strength.

It is said to be making a companion of heaven, as if offering it a cup of wine.

In ancient times, this was paramount.

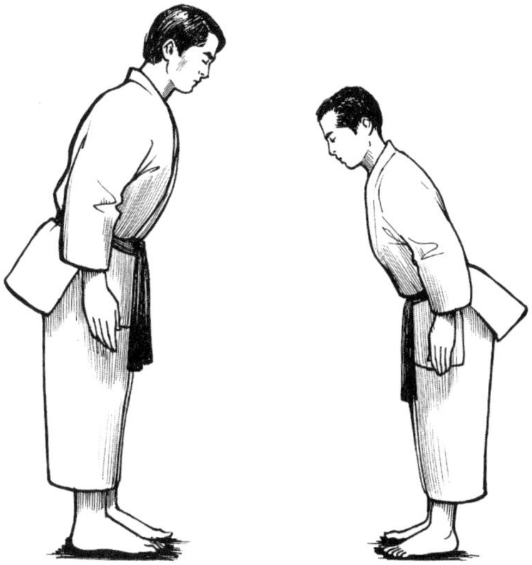

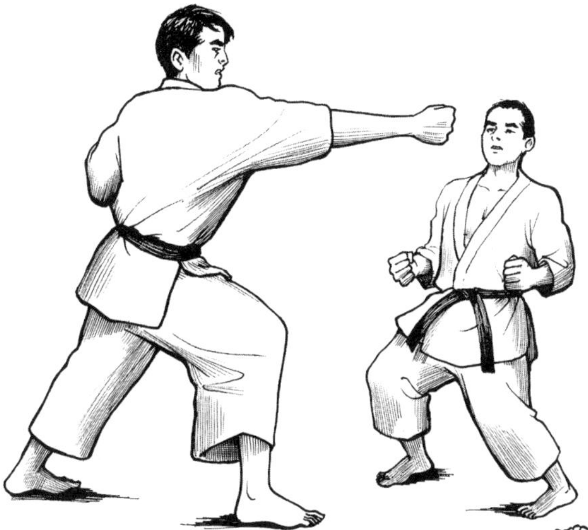

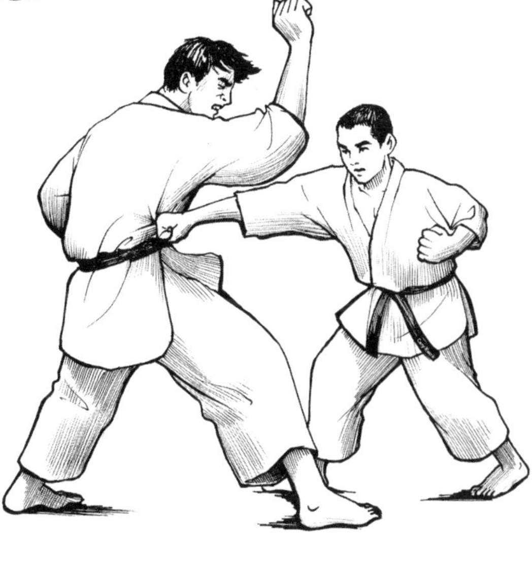

# 69

There is a saying for the use of weapons:

Do not be eager to act as the host; rather, act as the guest.

Do not be eager to advance an inch; rather, step back a foot.

This is said to be moving forward without doing so;

Striking and retreating without extending your elbow;

Seizing your opponent without a weapon,

And taking over while having no opponent at all.

There is no greater disaster than making light of your opponent;

Making light of your opponent almost always results in losing your treasures as easily as leaves fall from the trees.

Thus, when opponents meet with raised weapons,

The one who laments the fight will win.

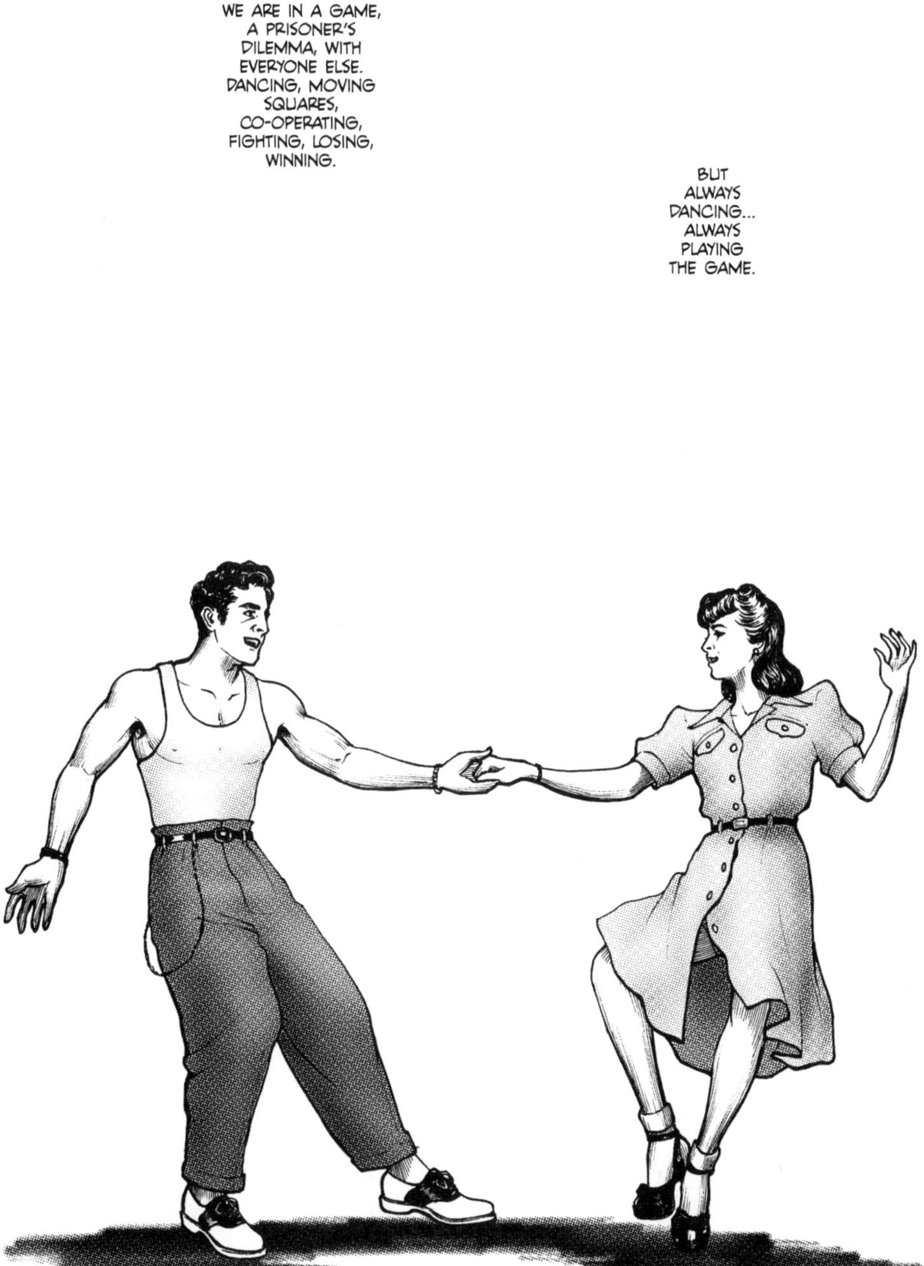
WE ARE IN A GAME, A PRISONER'S DILEMMA, WITH EVERYONE ELSE. DANCING, MOVING SQUARES, CO-OPERATING, FIGHTING, LOSING, WINNING.
BUT ALWAYS DANCING... ALWAYS PLAYING THE GAME.

# 70

My words are wonderfully easy to understand;

They are wonderfully easy to follow step by step.

But no one under heaven is capable of understanding them;

Nor can they follow them step by step.

Such words have a shrine for their guiding spirit;

Such actions have a lord who gives the orders.

Listen, people have no understanding whatsoever,

And so they do not understand me.

Those who understand me are few;

Those who follow my style are quite rare.

For this reason, the sage

Covers himself with rough clothes of animal fur,
and holds the stringed jewels close to his chest.

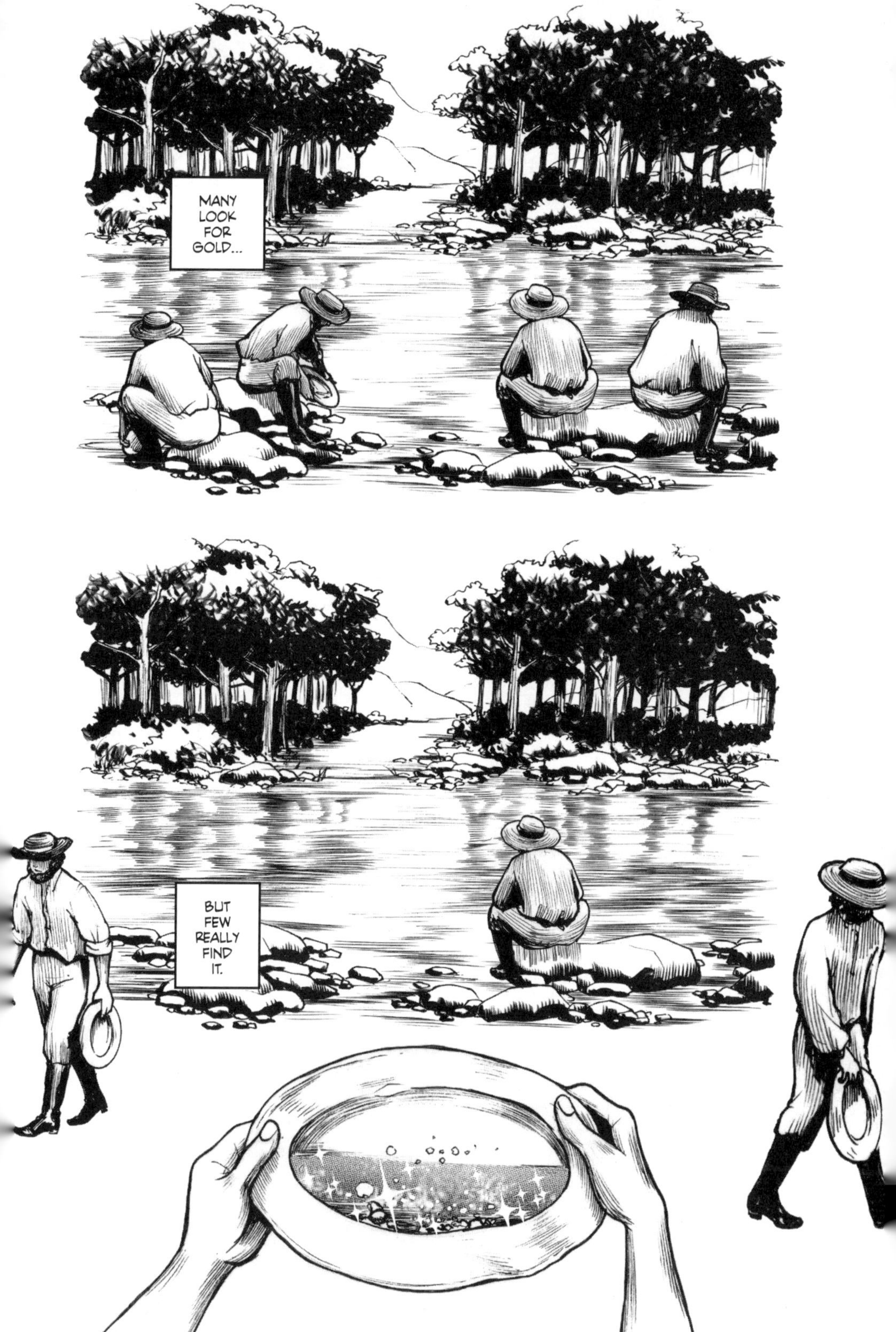
MANY LOOK FOR GOLD...
BUT FEW REALLY FIND IT.

# 71

Knowing that you do not know rests above the high-water mark.

Thinking that you know when you don't know, you are sick enough to be confined in bed.

Listen, just be sick of sickness,

And you will then not be sick.

The sage is not sick.

This is because he is sick of sickness.

Therefore, he is not sick.

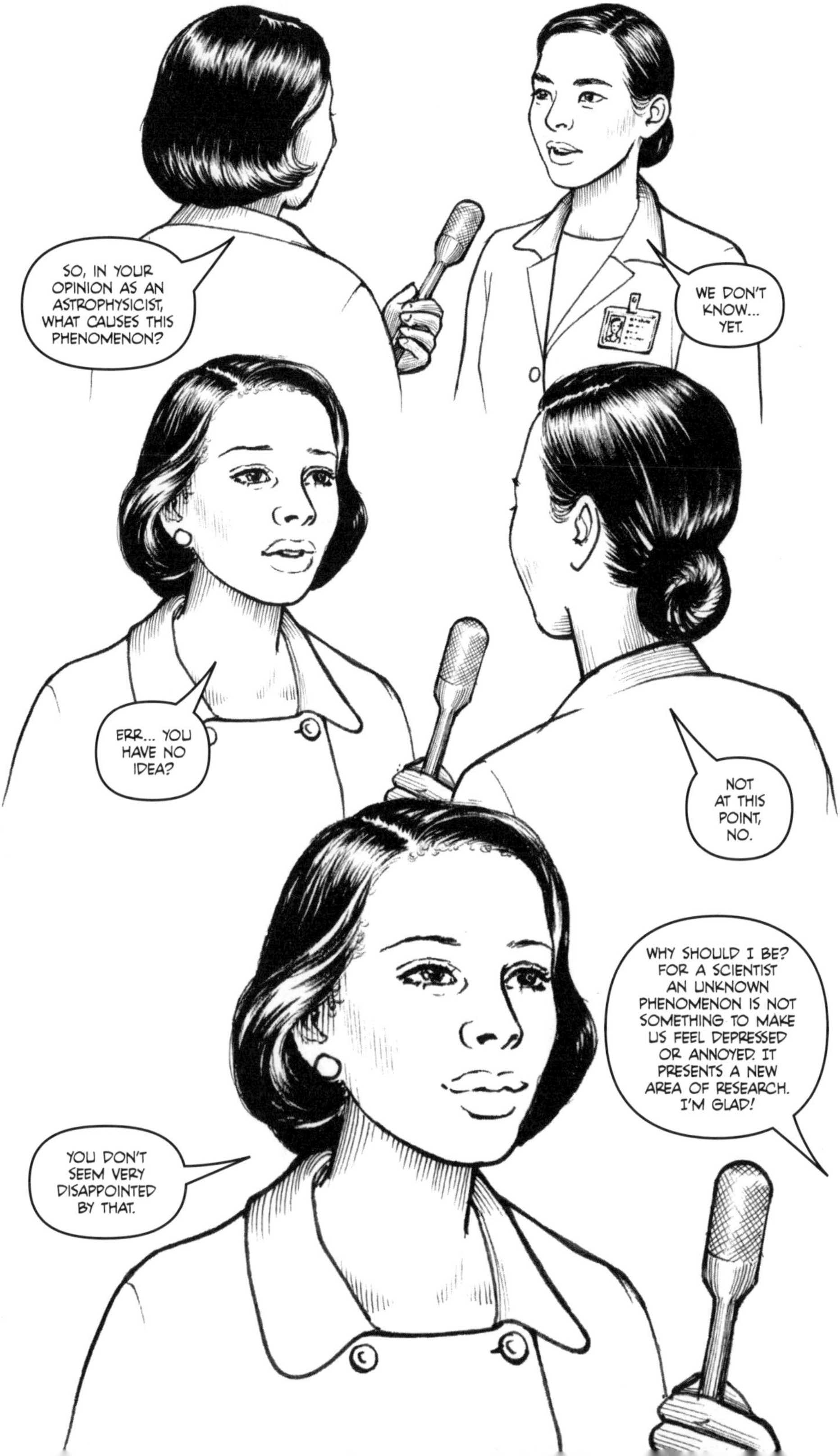
SO, IN YOUR OPINION AS AN ASTROPHYSICIST, WHAT CAUSES THIS PHENOMENON?
WE DON'T KNOW... YET.
ERR... YOU HAVE NO IDEA?
NOT AT THIS POINT, NO.
YOU DON'T SEEM VERY DISAPPOINTED BY THAT.
WHY SHOULD I BE? FOR A SCIENTIST AN UNKNOWN PHENOMENON IS NOT SOMETHING TO MAKE US FEEL DEPRESSED OR ANNOYED. IT PRESENTS A NEW AREA OF RESEARCH. I'M GLAD!

# 72

When the people do not respect authority, as they
might a demon holding a rod,

Then a greater authority will soon arrive reminiscent
of the days when women ruled the household.

The people should not make light of where they dwell;

Nor should they feel their lives restricted.

Listen, if they don't feel their lives to be restricted,

They will not be restricted.

Therefore the sage

    Knows himself well, but does not display himself;

    Loves himself, but does not make much of himself.

Thus, in each case he takes firm hold of the first and
avoids the last.

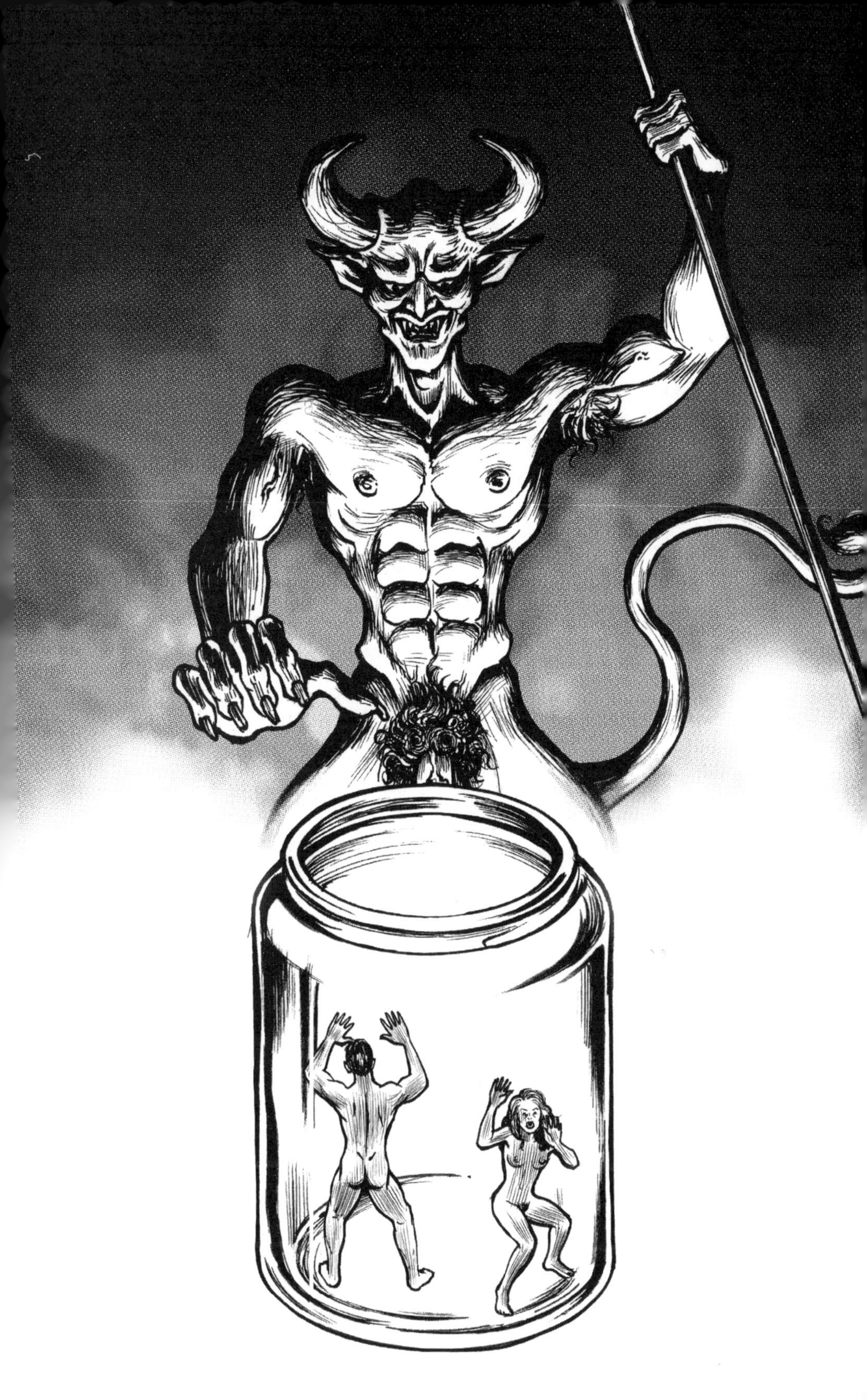

# 73

He who eagerly takes his courage into his own hands, will have his life cut off.

He who restrains his eagerness, will have life like gushing water.

Of these two things,

One prepares the ground for cultivation, the other suffocates life itself.

Therefore the sage is heavily suspicious and considers this difficult.

The Way of heaven

Does not contend, but is good at summoning its strength and standing its ground;

It does not speak, but is good at taking what is said to heart, and hitting the mark in response.

It does not wave you over to visit, but comes of its own accord.

It is loose and easy, but mulls things over well in silence.

Heaven's net is wonderfully vast and enveloping;

Though wide-meshed, nothing slips through.

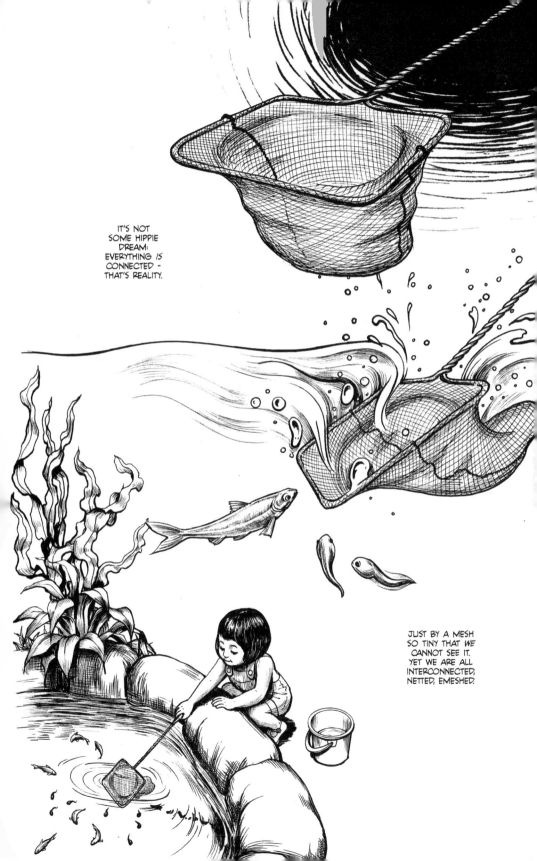

IT'S NOT SOME HIPPIE DREAM: EVERYTHING *IS* CONNECTED - THAT'S REALITY.

JUST BY A MESH SO TINY THAT *WE* CANNOT SEE IT. YET WE ARE ALL INTERCONNECTED, NETTED, EMESHED.

# 74

If the people have no fear of death, as they might of
armed demons,

Why should their eyes open wide with fear when death
is used as a threat?

Even if the people were constantly afraid of death,

And there were deviant characters to be shackled
and killed,

Who would be eager to do this?

It is an unchanging fact that there is an official
executioner at hand in charge of killing.

Listen, killing in place of the official executioner

Is like cutting and planing wood in place of a master
carpenter.

So take care: he is a rare man who cuts and planes
in place of a master carpenter,

And does not injure his own hand.

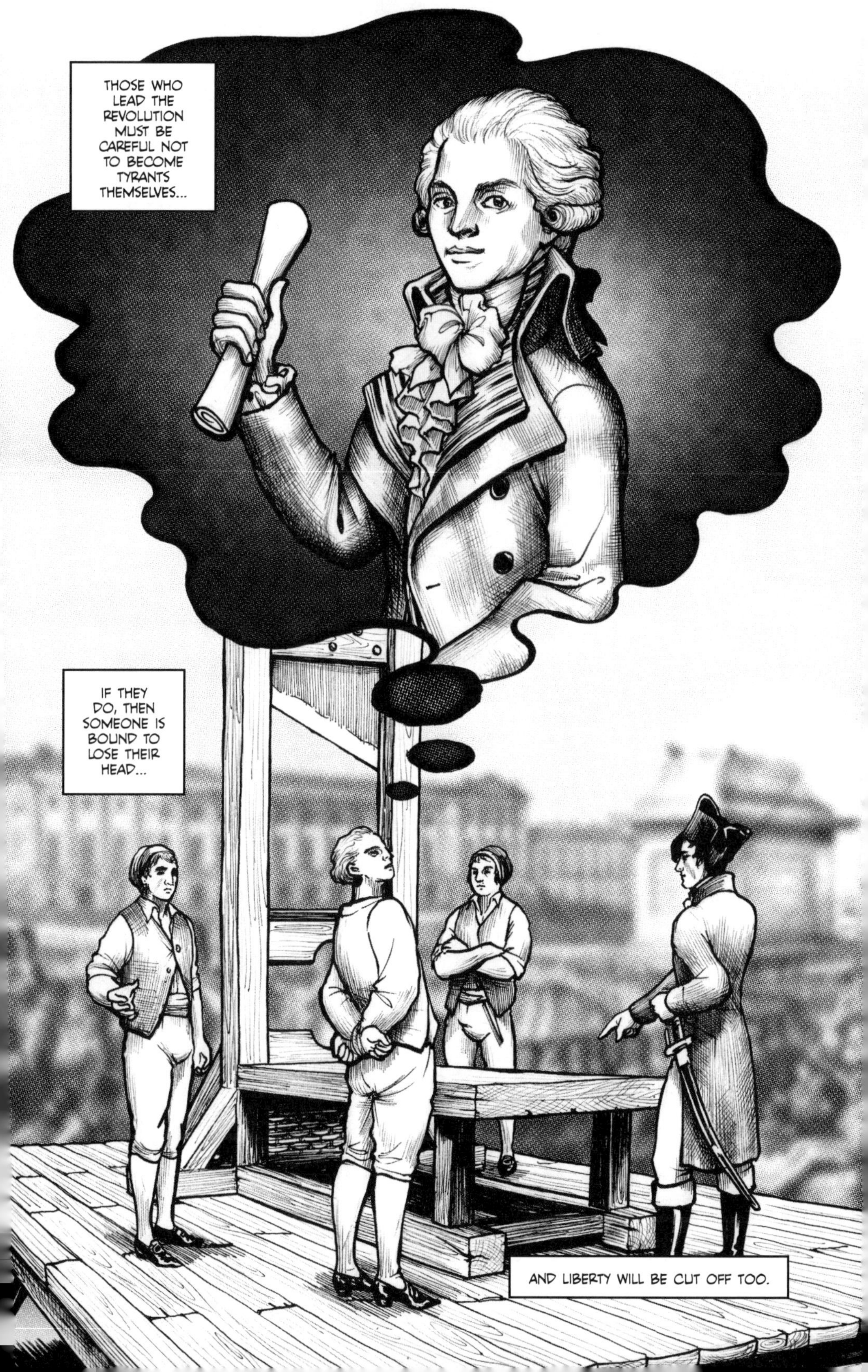
THOSE WHO LEAD THE REVOLUTION MUST BE CAREFUL NOT TO BECOME TYRANTS THEMSELVES...
IF THEY DO, THEN SOMEONE IS BOUND TO LOSE THEIR HEAD...
AND LIBERTY WILL BE CUT OFF TOO.

# 75

The people starve: there's famine and grains do not ripen.

This is because those above them feed excessively on those grains that are taxed.

For this reason, the people starve and face famine.

The people are difficult to manage:

This is because those above them are "doers" and fabricators.

For this reason the people are difficult to manage.

The people consider death no heavier than pulling a cart empty of baggage.

This is because they seek out life as though piling items one atop another.

For this reason they consider death no heavier than pulling an empty cart.

Listen, only the man who does not do things with "life" in mind,

Will have abundant respect for life itself.

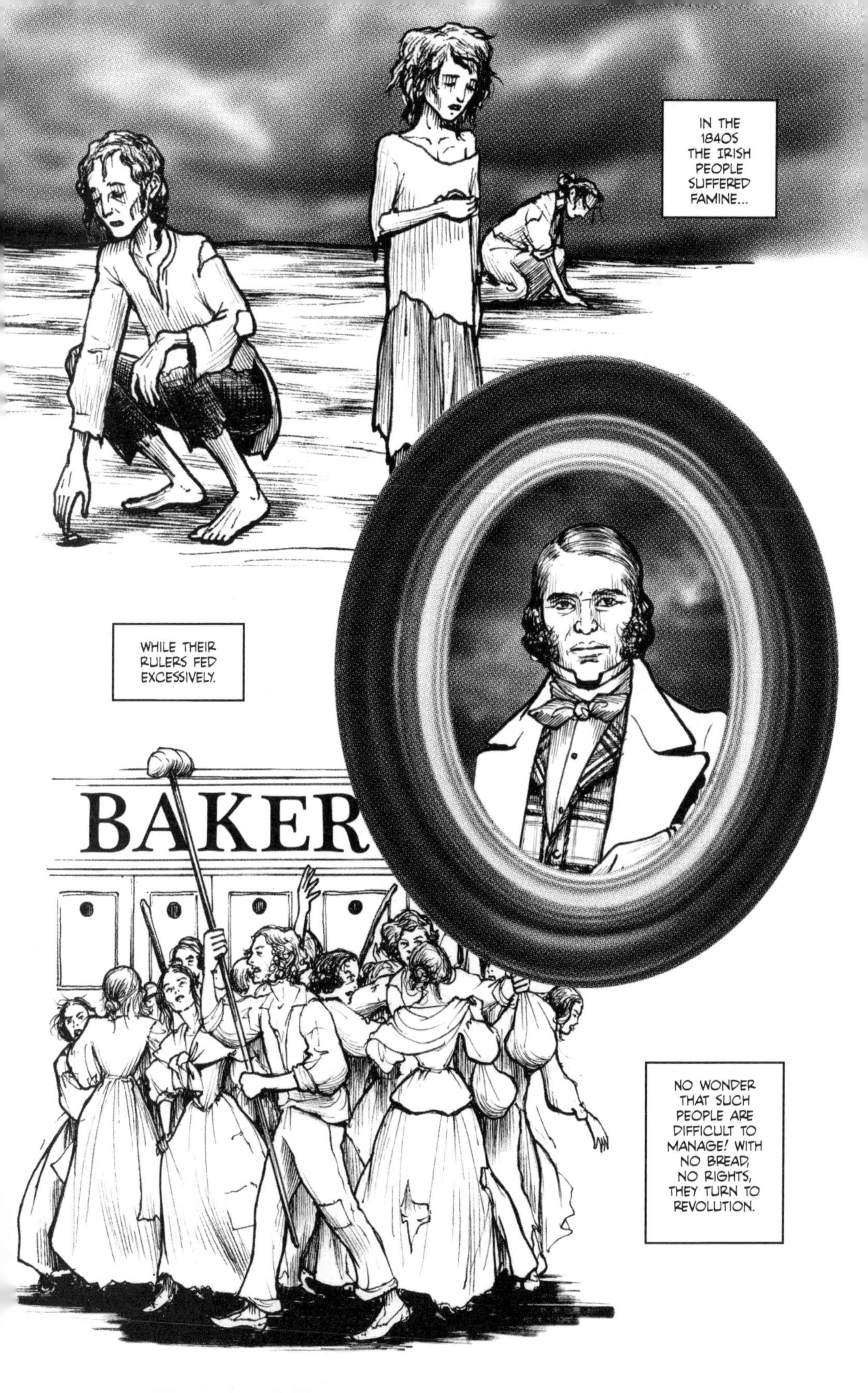
IN THE 1840S THE IRISH PEOPLE SUFFERED FAMINE...
WHILE THEIR RULERS FED EXCESSIVELY.
BAKER
NO WONDER THAT SUCH PEOPLE ARE DIFFICULT TO MANAGE! WITH NO BREAD, NO RIGHTS, THEY TURN TO REVOLUTION.

## 76

Man at birth is soft and flexible;

At death, he is rigid and as hard as clay.

While living, the Ten Thousand Things, especially the grasses and trees, are pliant and delicate;

In death, they are withered and desiccated like the branches atop an old tree.

Thus, the hard and rigid are the followers of death;

The pliant and flexible are the followers of life.

For this reason, if weapons are too rigid, they will not last.

If trees are too rigid, they will be cut down and used as furnishings.

The rigid and large reside below;

The pliant and flexible reside above.

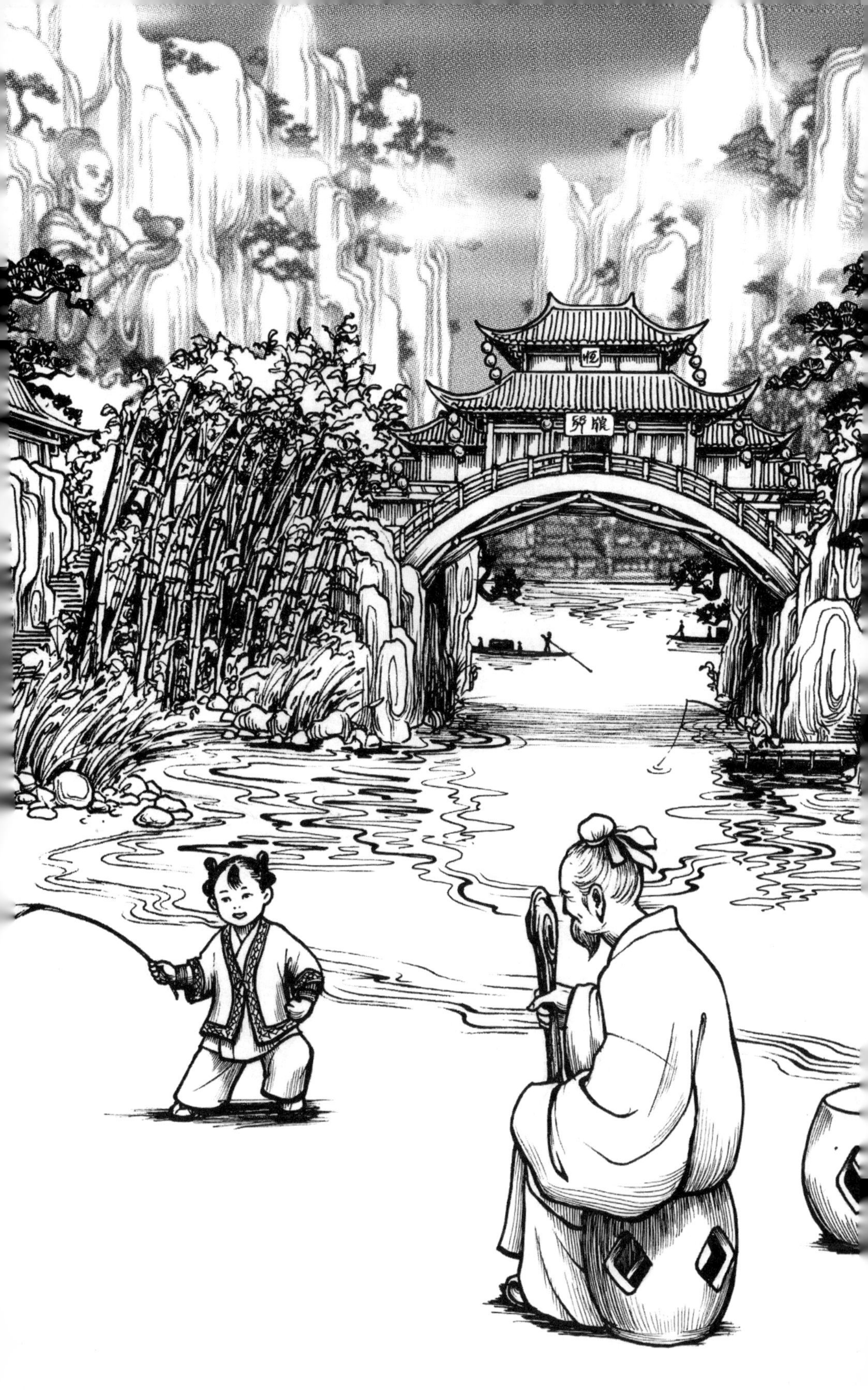

# 77

I suppose heaven's Way is much like drawing a bow:

The upper part is pulled down,

The lower part is pulled up.

Whatever is excessive, it decreases;

Whatever is insufficient, it supplements as you might mend a robe with a cloth.

The Way of heaven decreases what is excessive, and supplements the insufficient.

The Way of man is not so.

It decreases what is insufficient, and hands it over to the already excessive.

Who is capable of having excess and handing it over to all under heaven?

Only he who has the Way at hand.

For this reason, the sage

> Acts but relies on nothing;
>
> Gets his work done, but then moves on.
>
> He has no desire to show off his personal gifts.

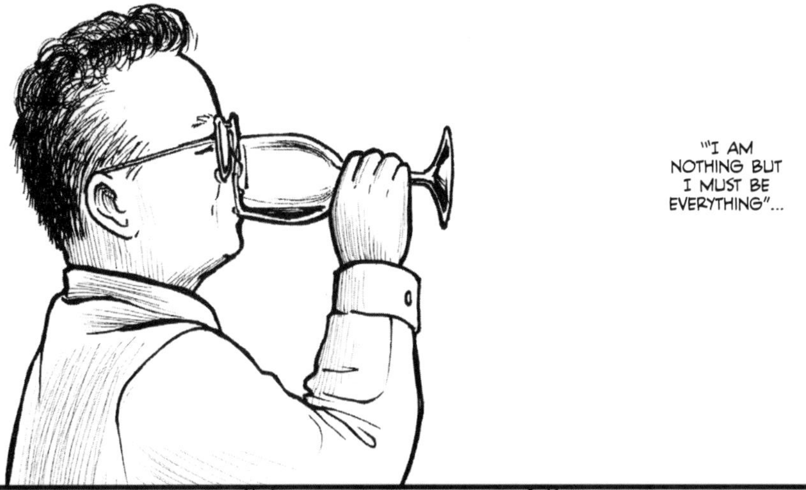
"'I AM NOTHING BUT I MUST BE EVERYTHING"...

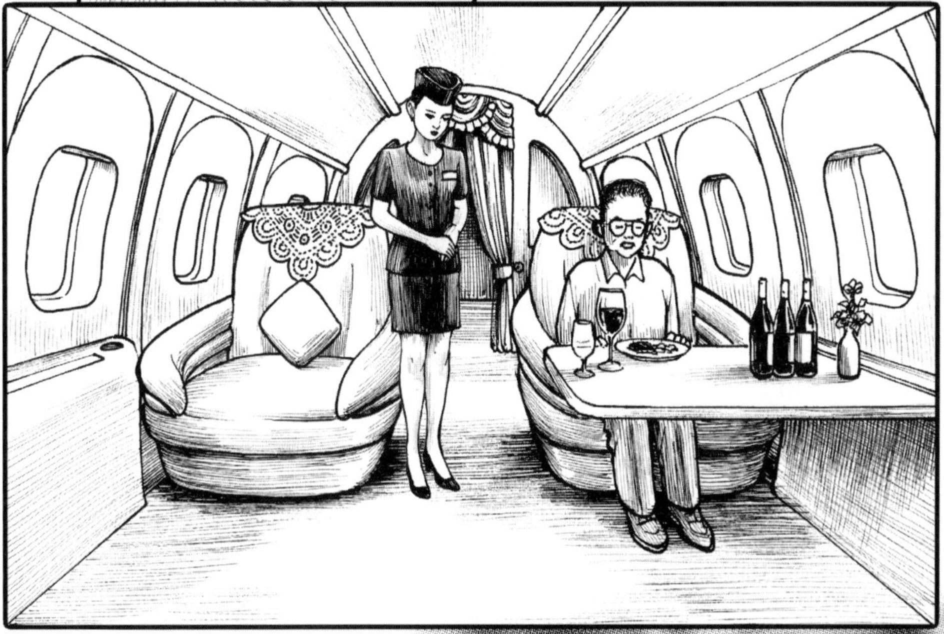

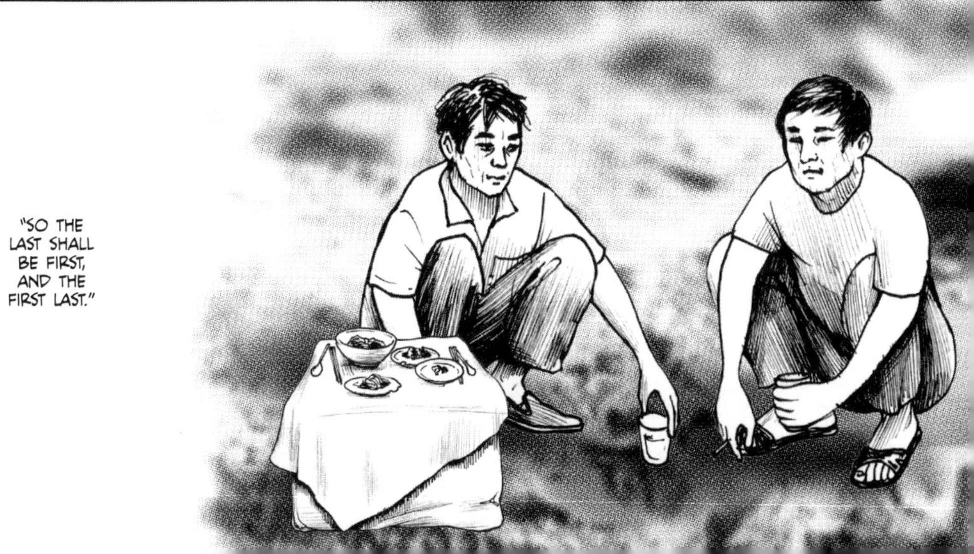
"SO THE LAST SHALL BE FIRST, AND THE FIRST LAST."

# 78

There is nothing under heaven as soft and pliant
as water;

Yet in striking against the hard and rigid,

There is nothing more capable of success.

This being as it is, there is nothing that could easily
take its place.

The pliant defeats the rigid;

The soft defeats the hard.

Under heaven, there is no one who does not know this,

But also no one capable of taking this rule step by step.

For this reason, the sage says,

> "Accepting responsibility for the state's blemishes:

> This is called being the main pillar of the shrine to
> the gods of the land.

> Accepting responsibility for the state's ill omens:

> This is called being king of all under heaven."

Unbiased words would appear to be their opposite.

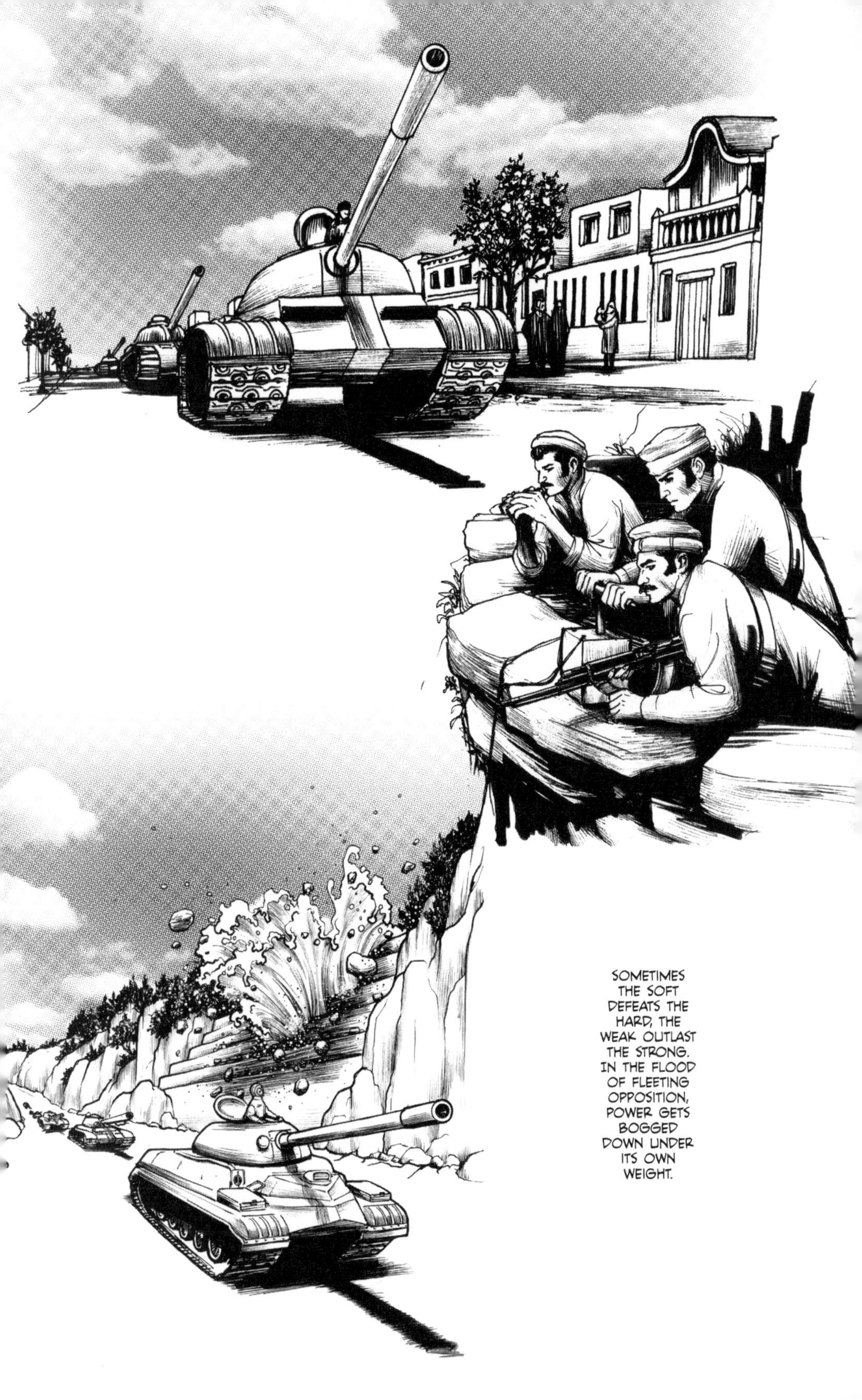
SOMETIMES THE SOFT DEFEATS THE HARD, THE WEAK OUTLAST THE STRONG. IN THE FLOOD OF FLEETING OPPOSITION, POWER GETS BOGGED DOWN UNDER ITS OWN WEIGHT.

# 79

In pacifying great rancor,

There will invariably be backbiting that remains.

What good can be made of this?

For this reason, the sage

> Grasps the left side of the contract,

> But does not importune others.

Those with virtue go by the rules of the contract;

Those without virtue go by what they can get away with.

The Way of heaven does not engage in nepotism,

But is unchangingly at the side of the good man.

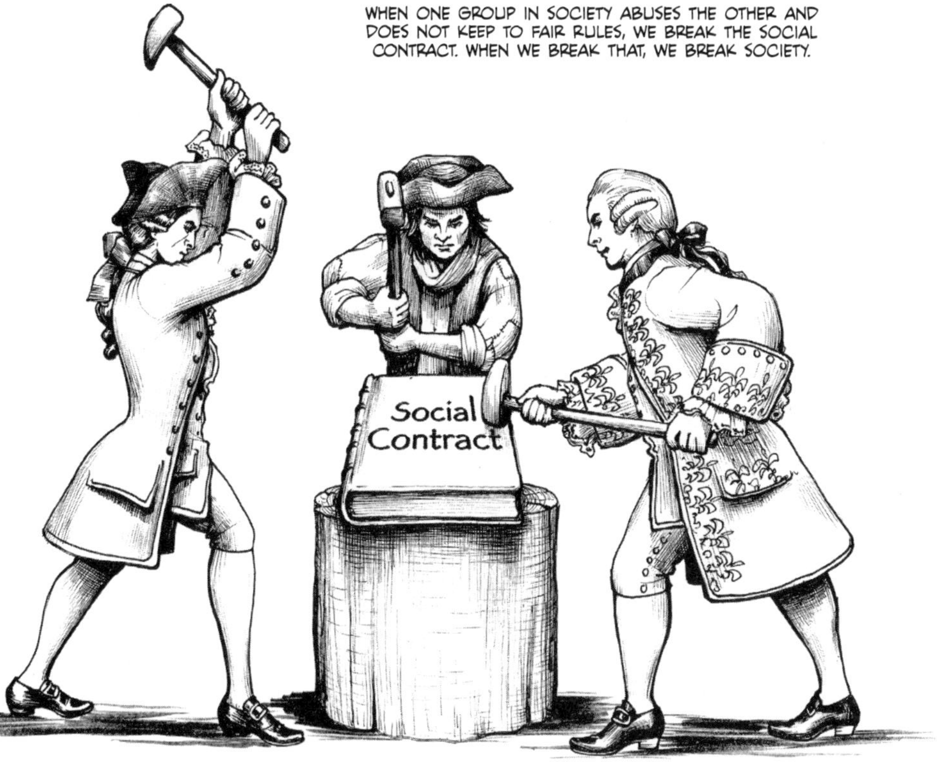
WHEN ONE GROUP IN SOCIETY ABUSES THE OTHER AND DOES NOT KEEP TO FAIR RULES, WE BREAK THE SOCIAL CONTRACT. WHEN WE BREAK THAT, WE BREAK SOCIETY.
Social Contract

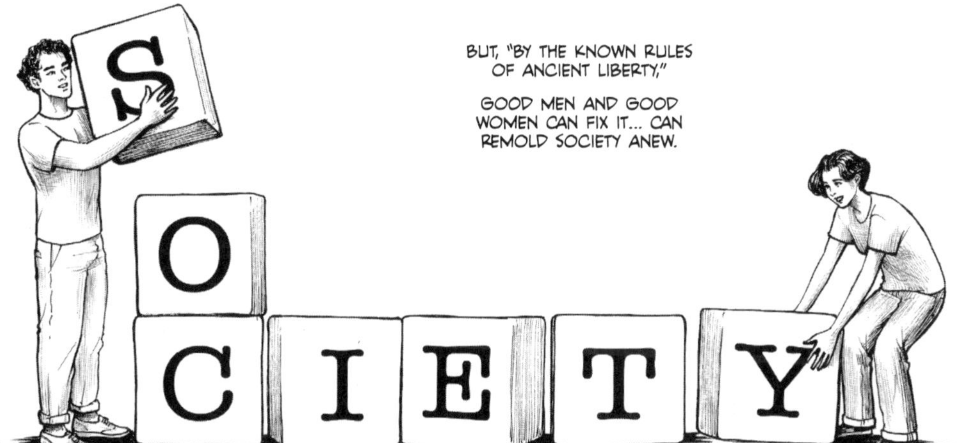
BUT, "BY THE KNOWN RULES OF ANCIENT LIBERTY,"
GOOD MEN AND GOOD WOMEN CAN FIX IT... CAN REMOLD SOCIETY ANEW.
S
O
C I E T Y

# 80

A small state with few people:

Though they have many convenient implements at hand, do not have them put into use.

Let the people treat death as weighty, and do not have them travel distant roads to settle elsewhere.

Though they have boats and drawn carriages,

There will be no occasion to ride in them.

Though armor and weapons be at hand,

There will be no occasion to set them out in martial display.

Have the people return to the custom of knotting cords and putting them to use.

Let them find their food tasty.

Let them find their clothing attractive.

Let them find their homes peaceful.

Let them take pleasure in their long-continued customs.

In this way, neighboring provinces may be within sight of each other,

But while the cries of the roosters and dogs of one may be heard in the other,

The people will reach old age and turn to dust

And never travel back and forth.

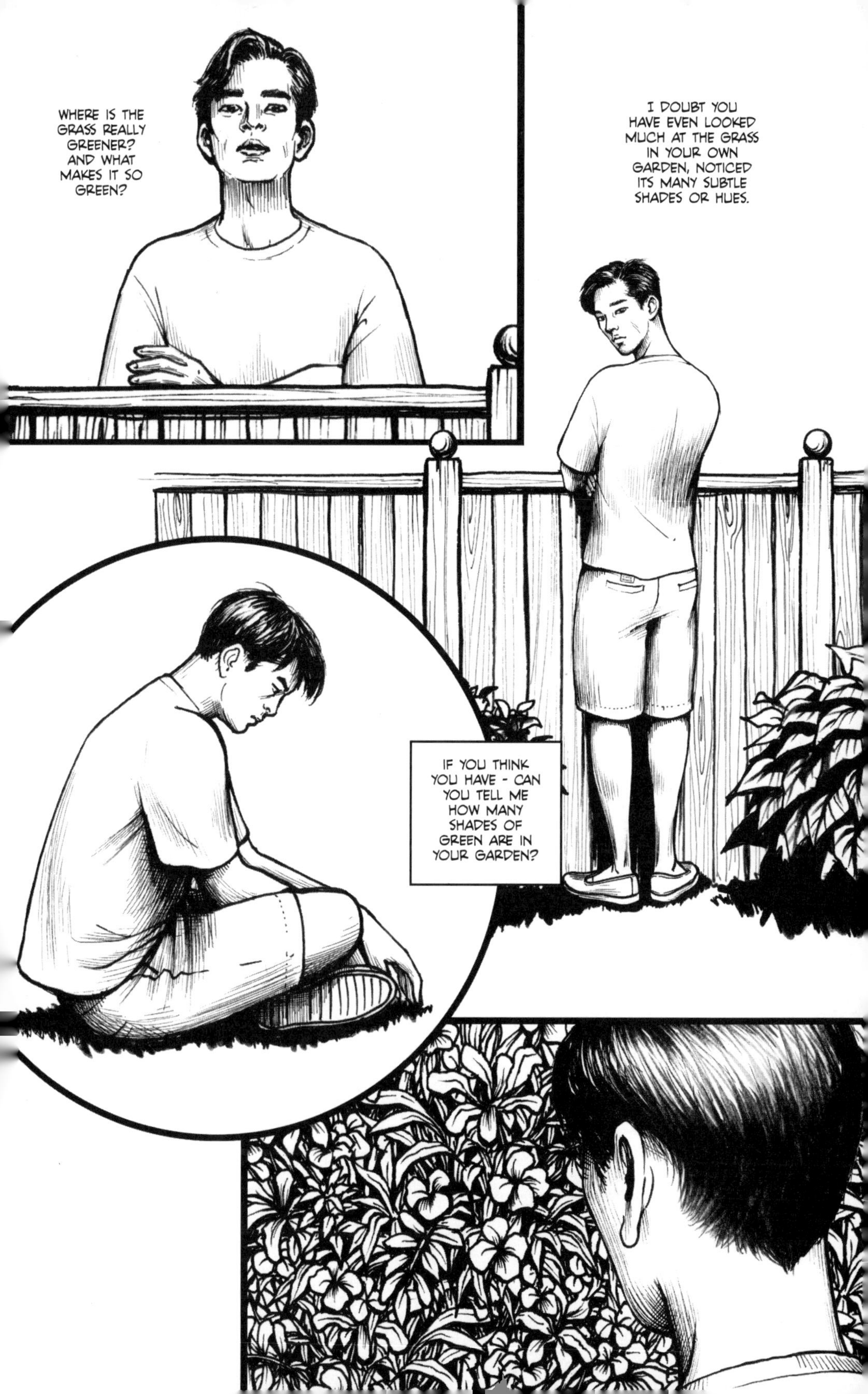
WHERE IS THE GRASS REALLY GREENER? AND WHAT MAKES IT SO GREEN?
I DOUBT YOU HAVE EVEN LOOKED MUCH AT THE GRASS IN YOUR OWN GARDEN, NOTICED ITS MANY SUBTLE SHADES OR HUES.
IF YOU THINK YOU HAVE - CAN YOU TELL ME HOW MANY SHADES OF GREEN ARE IN YOUR GARDEN?

# 81

Reliable words are not attractive;

Attractive words are not reliable.

Good people do not quibble;

Quibblers are not good people.

The knowing are not know-it-alls;

Know-it-alls are not knowing.

The sage does not hoard:

As much as he does for the sake of others,

He himself has all the more at hand.

The Way of heaven

Clears the ground for cultivation and does not hinder.

The Way of the sage

Is to act but not contend.

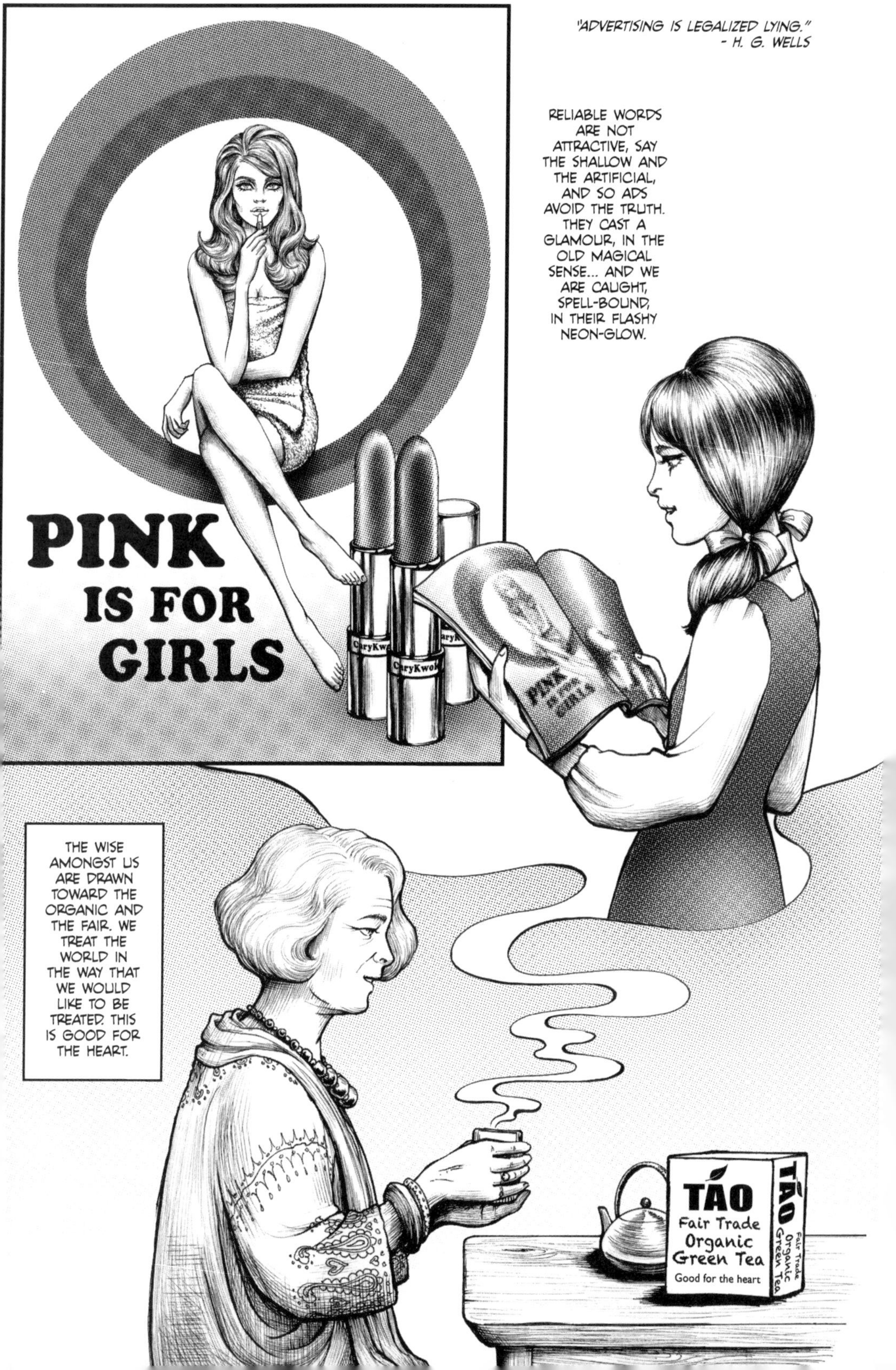
"ADVERTISING IS LEGALIZED LYING."
- H. G. WELLS
RELIABLE WORDS ARE NOT ATTRACTIVE, SAY THE SHALLOW AND THE ARTIFICIAL, AND SO ADS AVOID THE TRUTH. THEY CAST A GLAMOUR, IN THE OLD MAGICAL SENSE... AND WE ARE CAUGHT, SPELL-BOUND, IN THEIR FLASHY NEON-GLOW.
PINK IS FOR GIRLS
THE WISE AMONGST US ARE DRAWN TOWARD THE ORGANIC AND THE FAIR. WE TREAT THE WORLD IN THE WAY THAT WE WOULD LIKE TO BE TREATED. THIS IS GOOD FOR THE HEART.
TAO
Fair Trade
Organic
Green Tea
Good for the heart

# ABOUT THE AUTHOR AND ILLUSTRATOR

 **Sean Michael Wilson** is a Scottish writer living in Japan. He has published numerous graphic novels with a variety of publishers, which have been translated into twelve languages. In 2016, his book *Lafcadio Hearn's "The Faceless Ghost" and Other Macabre Tales from Japan* was nominated for the prestigious Eisner Award for best adaptation and received a medal from the Independent Publisher Book Awards. In 2017, his book *Secrets of the Ninja* won an International Manga Award from the Japanese government; he is the first British person to receive this award.

 **Cary Kwok** is a London-based artist who has received wide acclaim for his unique style of ballpoint pen art. Born and raised in Hong Kong, he studied at Central Saint Martins College of Art and Design and holds a Master of Arts degree in fashion design. Cary's artwork is represented by Herald St Gallery in London and has been exhibited internationally in New York, Miami, Tokyo, Geneva, Zurich, and more.